The Mindful Money Mentality

How To Find Balance in Your Financial Future

by Holly P. Thomas, CFP®

Porchview Publishing LLC
2202 N West Shore Blvd., Suite 200
Tampa, FL 33607 USA
porchviewpublishing@gmail.com

The stories and anecdotes in this book are based on true experiences. However, all names are pseudonyms, some stories are compilations, and some situations have been changed slightly for educational purposes or to protect the privacy of and confidential relationship with those involved.

This book is designed to provide accurate and authoritative information in regard to the subject matter covered. It is not intended to provide investment advisory, legal, tax, accounting, or financial planning services. Individual financial situations are unique, and therefore, any and all financial, tax, legal or investment questions must be addressed by the appropriate professional. If you do not wish to be bound by the above, you may return this book to the publisher for a full refund.

Design by Jenna Kusmierek

A portion of the net income from sales of The Mindful Money Mentality will be donated by the author to charities supporting mental health and financial literacy.

ISBN: 978-0-9888049-0-6

Issued also in electronic format

Printed in the United States of America

Library of Congress Cataloging-in-Publication Data
Thomas, Holly P.
The mindful money mentality: how to find balance in your financial future / Holly Thomas – 1st ed.
ISBN: 978-0-9888049-0-6
1. Finance, Personal – Psychological aspects.
2013915125

Table of Contents

Introduction ix

PART 1: Money and You 1

CHAPTER 1: This Book and You 3

Who Is This Book For? 3

How to Use this Book 10

CHAPTER 2: Minding Our Money Messages 13

CHAPTER 3: Integrating the Money Principles 25

CHAPTER 4: Applying Mindfulness in Practice 39

Savings Decisions 39

Where Do You Want Your Money To Take You? 45

Decisions About Sharing 69

Estate Planning 73

Unplanned Sharing: Lending versus Giving 75

PART II: Mindful Money Management and You 79

CHAPTER 5: Mindful Financial Planning and Investing 81

First Principle: Get the Mix Right 86

Second Principle: Let It Stew 87

Third Principle: Own All, Not Some 87

Fourth Principle: Own Some, Not All 91

Fifth Principle: Rebalance Regardless Regularly 99

CHAPTER 6: Delegating Money Management 101

Personal Experience with Professionals 102

A 5-Point Test for Finding Financial Professionals 105

Your Part 138

CHAPTER 7: Emotional Threats to Mindfulness 143

Behavioral Economics and Psychology 144

Biases: Rational versus Stupid 149

Remedies for Natural Emotional Reactions 188

CHAPTER 8: Upholding a Mindful Money Mentality 197

Your Rights and Responsibilities 200

How Will You Know You Made the Right Decisions? 203

Resources and Reading List 207

Acknowledgments 217

Holly Thomas' book should be required reading for anyone embarking on developing a "wealth planning roadmap", whether with or without professional guidance, as well as those revisiting their current wealth management strategies. Despite having worked in the financial services and wealth management industry for nearly four decades, I found myself reflecting on decisions I've made and evaluating decisions I likely need to make. Well written and easily understandable, the material allows readers to step back and mull over many important concepts. A must read.

Richard Sincere, Founder and CEO of Sincere & Co., LLC

Holly has a particular talent for asking insightful, thought-provoking questions. She's woven a series of self-assessment questions throughout The Mindful Money Mentality. Read the book with a pad and pen nearby, and do pause to engage with the questions she asks. Allow yourself to explore any other questions these evoke. You'll find that these questions will trigger a gentle yet fruitful inner dialogue, which may lead to some tremendous self-money-discovery. Having a clear understanding of your 'internal money self' makes for much more meaningful external money decisions. As I always tell my clients: there are no right or wrong money decisions; there are only money decisions which are right or wrong for you. Holly's book is an excellent guide and tool to help you get clear about what is most meaningful and right for you.

Jennifer Lazarus, CFP®, Lazarus Financial Planning

Holly has an innate ability to get inside your mind and help you to face your investment decisions. Her powerful and insightful book caused me to be "mindful" of my relationship with money, my risk tolerance, and my perception of "enough" to make better educated choices for my entire financial lifestyle as well as who is best to help me manage it all! Holly opens up your eyes to the inside of the Investment Industry and you as an individual – a must read for your balanced financial future!

Terry Lubotsky, MSed, Consultant, Facilitator, Speaker, Coach & Author

Introduction

"In every moment, we find ourselves at the crossroad of here and now. But when the cloud of forgetfulness over where we are now sets in, in that very moment we get lost.... and ... fall into a robotlike way of seeing and thinking and doing. In these moments, we break contact with what is deepest in ourselves and affords us perhaps our greatest opportunities for creativity, learning, and growing. ....Not knowing that you are even in such a dream is what the Buddhists call 'ignorance,' or mindlessness. Being in touch with this not knowing is called 'mindfulness."

~ Jon Kabat-Zinn, Wherever You Go, There You Are, p. xv.

My hope for this book is that you begin to cultivate "mindfulness" about your relationship with money. For many of us, unconsciously or not, money takes on iconic status and becomes something of which we can never have enough. In Kabat-Zinn's "robotlike way," we work and save and spend and work while money flows in and out of our lives without direction, planning, thought, or purpose. Following this way to the end of our lives can be disastrous. There comes a point where some of us do indeed have enough. But if we don't recognize it, we stand to lose time and experience, and foster relationships that do not give us joy.

I hope this book takes you to a new place, where money is not your benchmark, but becomes a tool that enables you to live the life you truly want.

PART I

MONEY AND YOU

1

This Book and You

"Your vision will become clear only when you can look into your own heart." ~ Carl Jung

Who Is This Book For?

Our society leads us to believe that having more money will free us from difficult choices. In fact, though, even those with "enough" money struggle with decisions about it—spending it, saving it, sharing it, investing it, and hiring professional help to manage it.

In my work as a Certified Financial Planner®, I encounter people preparing for, or transitioning into, the next chapter in their lives. Some have kids going to college, some want a new career, and some are ready to exit the workforce.

I became intrigued with so-called "successful savers"—people who choose to make saving a priority in their financial lives but still find plenty to worry about. They might save through their employers' retirement plans, or by setting aside an inheritance, receiving a settlement, making regular contributions to an investment account or

IRA, or by building a business. They think they will probably have "enough," but they aren't sure.

They discover that the skills necessary for success at saving money are not the same as the skills needed for spending it, sharing it, investing it, and hiring help with it. It's theirs to use — but it's also theirs to lose. They want to know, "How can I make sure I don't screw this up?"

"Screwing up" seems to be one of the biggest fears we all face. If there are 50 ways to leave your lover, there must be 50,000 ways to run out of money.

And in tough financial times, when you open your statement and see that years of hard-earned savings have evaporated, it is easy and natural to fear the worst, to begin thinking you will never be able to live the life you want.

Unfortunately, the very real risks we take as we plan for the future, combined with our fear about it, can lead us to an unbalanced relationship with money, along with less than optimal decisions. Many good savers grow dependent on money—not on using it, but on having it. The bottom line on the account statement represents security. I know how hard it can be to let that go.

A Little Background

As a behavioral economist (in a field that studies the psychology of personal economic decisions), I have a keen interest in our relationships with money. I care about maximizing its usefulness as a tool rather than elevating its status as an end. But for much of my life, I had those two reversed. I did my own financial planning backwards. I put the pursuit of money first, life second, and myself last. In other words, I floated in a fog about my attachment to money, swept along by society's encouragement and my own beliefs. My money mentality was not aware, awake, or intentional. It was unconscious. It was anything but mindful.

I was one of those successful savers. Starting when I was a teenager, I kept track of every penny I spent. I could not wait until my 21st birthday so I could start contributing to my employer's 401(k).

In my 20s and 30s, I focused on money as an end, determined to define my success as a person by the amount of money I made. As a result, I made some choices that caused me, and those around me, to suffer unnecessarily. I fretted over how much essential things cost. It hurt me to spend on myself for anything nice, much less on anybody else. I now realize that having money was a way to feel good about myself. In my mind, my earnings defined my success as a person. This is the area where I was most imbalanced, and I regret some of the decisions I made then.

After college, I joined a Miami bank training program. I saw that most of the trainees chose to live in a new suburban complex requiring a Metro commute. I chose to live in cheaper North Miami, only ten minutes from downtown, proud that I was saving on rent, gas, and Metro fares. The building was newly renovated but occupied mostly by taxi drivers who kept odd hours, and the crime rate was higher in my neighborhood. My car was broken into in the parking garage. I did not get much exercise because, as a 5-foot-3-inch 20-year-old, I didn't feel safe going outside.

While my coworkers were discussing the fun evenings they had had at south Miami restaurants, I thought, "Bah, humbug!" I was proud not to "waste" my money on frivolities. Over the seven-month training program, I not only did not exercise enough, I unconsciously distanced myself from the camaraderie of the other trainees. While I eventually fixed the exercise deficiency later in life, the friendships I might have had and enjoyed today are absent.

It was not easy for me to accept that what you have is not who you are. I didn't understand that if you looked to your net worth to find your self-worth, your net worth would never be high enough. It was a vicious cycle: I never felt good enough, so clearly I didn't have enough; when I had more, I still didn't feel good enough, so clearly I still didn't have enough, and so on.

When I was 40, my then-employer merged with another company, and the new bank had very different priorities. A brokerage company had been trying to recruit me, so as part of the decision to make a jump, I ran a financial analysis to see how much risk my husband and I could take on.

I told him, "I have done these calculations six ways to Sunday. It appears that right now, if we do not save another dime, when we are 60 we are guaranteed a double-wide mobile home and early-bird specials at Denny's." I was being facetious, but it was clear to me that this was not good enough. We would need to keep working and saving for more.

To my surprise, he said, "Sounds good!"

I had always assumed that I would have to maximize my earnings as much as possible until age 60 because that was what everyone was supposed to do. Suddenly I had the space to step back and think: what do we really need? I thought: "I guess it's not too bad to be 40 and know we have at least what we have now. In fact, if I had to, I could definitely live with that."

I felt liberated. Suddenly I had a world of choices before me.

When I began to understand the meaning of "enough," the pursuit of money ceased to control me. As a result of changing my money mentality, I was able to start my own business, write this book, and realize I would rather be debt-free than live in a big house; I could spend more time on my new porch, and I could make myriad decisions from a position of security and confidence, rather than pursuing the vague goal of achieving another dollar without knowing why.

Money is not the destination; it is merely the vehicle. The hardest work for me was figuring out what life I wanted to live to be happy. Once that became clear, the tough decisions fell into place. If I had figured out what I wanted first, I might have saved myself a couple of decades of unnecessary work and worry. (The irony is, those years probably shortened my life, which is one way to avoid running out of money!)

Applying Mindfulness in Practice

Awakening to money's proper role in your life is the first step. Next is applying that mindfulness in planning, and then maintaining it in the face of emotional distraction. This book will walk you through the steps for acquiring a mindful money mentality.

Once we have a mindful money mentality, we have the challenge of implementing it in real-life decisions. Saving, spending, sharing, and investing choices can be made more intentionally and thoughtfully. But even with more consciousness in our decision-making, some will seek the services of a financial professional. While Part I of this book helps you reach a mindful money mentality, Part II helps you learn how to look for and engage the help of competent, ethical, and mindful professionals.

There is a prescribed six-step financial planning process that providers generally use:

Step 1: Define what financial planning services are to be provided to the client, how the planner will be paid, and for how long.

Step 2: Find out the client's financial profile, including goals.

Step 3: Analyze and evaluate data.

Step 4: Develop recommendations and options.

Step 5: Implement the options chosen.

Step 6: Monitor on a regular basis.

When I first became a financial planner, these steps made perfect sense to me. My job was to collect data, analyze it, apply my knowledge and expertise to it, then spit out a list of recommendations for what to do with it. After the client selected my recommendations, then I would work my magic implementing them. Every time we met, I could show the client more data and numbers.

But who was this six-step process really about? Me, me, me, the all-knowing expert planner! And the client? A source of "data." You, the client, would provide data. I, the expert, would then show you my stuff. You'd sit back and marvel. Sound good?

The six-step process is a good start for beginning planners. (It certainly tops "Step 1: Ask the client how many children he or she has. Step 2: Sell an insurance product.") But at no real point in this basic planning process is there a two-way conversation. The communication is all one-way, and the client, you, can take it or leave it. In my private banking career, I dealt with savvy, wealthy people. They did not take it. They questioned it. And then, so did I.

How could the financial planning process be more mindful? Perhaps it could look something like the outline for this book:

1. Discover your historical relationship with money. Evaluate your money messages, flashpoints, beliefs, and habits. (Chapter 2)

2. Integrate what you've discovered about your past messages and beliefs with your current personal values and goals for the future. (Chapter 3)

3. Apply your values to specific decisions about saving, spending, and sharing. (Chapter 4)

4. Design an investing plan that maximizes your odds of success while taking the minimum risk necessary. (Chapter 5)

5. If you need help with Step 4, interview and hire outside investment professionals to assist you. (Chapter 6)

6. Build your defenses against common emotional obstacles to successful implementation of the plans. (Chapter 7)

7. Put your plan into action and honor what you've learned. Monitor changes in family, legal, tax, and financial situations and keep professionals, if any, informed. Revisit plans, rebalance, and review professional relationships annually. Stay mindful, but let your money work for you rather than the other way around. (Chapter 8)

Not everyone is prepared to answer the introspective questions required to become more mindful. When I ask them in person, some clients respond with a stunned, silent stare. Some would prefer to skip that part. I found that people who have not answered these questions tend to think of life as a zero-sum game of scarcity, a competition where you must lose if I am to win. Ironically, people who are clear about exactly what they want, and have a plan to get there, view the world as far more abundant.

A *mindful* money mentality is an *abundance* mentality.

Mindful: adj.
1. Tending toward awareness and appreciation.
2. Marked by comprehension, cognizance, and perception.
3. Cautiously attentive. (**Roget's II: The New Thesaurus,** Houghton Mifflin, 1980).

How to Use this Book

The mission of this book is to guide you through a process of discovering the highest and best use of money in your life, your approach to money decisions, and how you can protect a lifetime of savings from both sudden threats and gradual ones. By the end of the book, you will be better equipped to make decisions about saving, spending, sharing, investing, and hiring professional help—with fewer emotional obstacles.

Using the Self-Assessments in each chapter, you will discover your unique money strengths and weaknesses that have evolved through your money history. You will become aware of how your brain works during money decisions. You will have the foundation of a mindful saving, spending, sharing, and investing plan. You will understand when to ask for professional help and how to evaluate which professionals are acting in your best interests. You will find the right balance for spending, saving, investing, and sharing by clarifying what you want money for in the first place.

If you do decide to interview financial professionals, you can use your Self-Assessments to give candidate professionals an idea of who you are with money and what you need and want from money. The better candidates will relish your work and be intrigued. The weaker ones won't pay it much attention. It will be clear which is which.

The answers to some of your questions will come easily, while others may take time. The more meaningful you make your answers, the more satisfying your results will be by the end. The result of this process will be to increase your confidence in your money as the vessel that will get you to your destination safely. Along the way, your job is to enjoy the journey.

2

Minding Our Money Messages

"That the birds of worry and care fly above your head, this you cannot change. But that they build nests in your hair, this you can prevent."
~Chinese proverb

We all have money messages. Some serve us well, while others could use some work. To become more mindful, we need to uncover and explore these messages—essentially, our underlying beliefs—and where they come from, and whether they are helping or hindering us. Many of us are not even aware of these messages because they are such an integral part of who we are.

It's common to harbor feelings of regret or guilt over past money decisions. Some people have splurged on a large house. Others have bought an investment that soured. Some have helped a friend or relative start a business that failed. For some, the decision was a one-time mistake. Others discover that their poor money decisions seem to follow a lifelong pattern. They wonder why they continue to make the same regrettable decisions over and over. They think their money history means they are "not good with money."

It can be easy to group ourselves and those around us into categories: "good with money" and "not good with money." Even the wealthiest people in the world have money concerns that disturb their lives. Does being wealthy mean you are "good with money"? Or does it just mean you have a lot of it? Imagine: some wealthy people have a lot of something that makes them miserable. And many poor people in the world, with less on their minds and in their wallets, lead far happier lives.

One of the goals of the workshops I give is to understand how the beliefs and behaviors of the people around us—especially when we are children—form messages about our relationship with money. Those messages can be intensified by certain financial events or experiences and then reinforced by both healthy and unhealthy money habits. What follows here is a look at how we begin to become mindful of our money beliefs.

Beliefs

Before my workshops begin, I often put a series of posters on the walls, each poster showing a different money message:

- Waste not, want not.
- Easy come, easy go.
- Money is evil.
- If you have money, don't tell anyone.
- Poverty is a virtue.
- Better to give than to receive.
- Money is not important.
- There will always be enough.

- There will never be enough.
- Think about the poor starving children in....
- A penny saved is a penny earned.
- Do you think money grows on trees?
- You deserve the best.
- Just because everyone else has something doesn't mean you have to.
- If I could just win the lottery, everything would be okay.
- They are poor because they are lazy.
- Money brings you happiness.
- There is only so much money in the world.
- Only money made by hard labor is worth having.
- Don't spend money.
- You can't take it with you.

After we settle in, I ask the participants to walk around the room and read the messages. Then I ask them to reflect upon which authority figures in their lives (mom, dad, grandparents, minister, rabbi, elementary teacher, coach, etc.) could be identified with the messages. This helps them begin to understand the different sources of their deeply held beliefs.

I then split the participants into groups and give each a list of fictional scenarios. I ask each group to brainstorm the messages each scenario might convey to a child.

- When you went out to eat in a restaurant, your mother always ordered the least expensive item on the menu and your father always ordered everything from soup to nuts.

- Your family had a bottle for extra change and every night everyone put their change into the bottle to save for something special.

- There was a lot of yelling and accusations when someone was paying the bills.

- Your mother always looked for bargains, including in consignment shops, when she shopped for a special-occasion one-time outfit.

- Your mother was usually very careful about spending money but she would go all out for a special occasion.

- Your father bought a brand new car every year but would not help you pay for college.

- One parent didn't live with your family but always bought you special gifts.

- Your uncle lived with your family for months at a time. Although your mom complained that he ate everything in sight but didn't help with the expenses, she never said anything to him.

- Your father frequently came home from a sale with another tool or gadget for his workshop. Most of his buys stayed in the boxes and he rarely used them.

- Your widowed aunt lived in a big but deteriorating house, drove an old car, and never bought new clothes, but she made large donations to her late husband's alma mater.

- Your mother told you not to tell your father how much your new shoes cost.

- One parent wanted to buy a house and the other wanted to stay in an apartment.

One outcome of this exercise is that participants realize that we all grow up with different money messages. During interactions with others during a money decision—whether it's a family member or a financial professional—it helps to remember and appreciate that they are coming from a unique set of beliefs. Our sets of beliefs may be similar, but they are rarely exactly the same. The more mindful we are of these differing beliefs, the smoother such conversations tend to go. [1]

The Media

The media play a large role in forming our money messages. One important reason why you may not feel confident about money is that the media and their customers—financial companies who advertise—have a vested interest in keeping us worried. They do this by encouraging us to ask the wrong questions, like "How much money do you need to have to have enough?" or "How much income can you get?" Or, rephrased in recent years, "What's your Number?"

Everyone fears unpleasant surprises, and we tend to believe our best defense against them is to feel tuned-in. But imagine if every TV and internet channel told us that unpleasant surprises would occur regardless of how informed we think we are, and therefore the best idea would be to put a mindful financial plan in place for your lifestyle and then take your best friend fishing?

Some media, but not all, create the illusion that finances and money are so complex and confusing that you need multiple academic degrees and a century of experience to understand and handle them. The money message that is conveyed makes people feel "stupid" about money.

Some people feel "stupid" because they pick up a Wall Street Journal and cannot understand every word of it. Being knowledgeable about finance is certainly important, but it isn't necessary for financial success that you understand, for example, the market for currency derivatives or the leverage ratios of REITs. (Just because a patient can't comprehend endocrinology in the Harvard Medical Review does not mean he or she is unable to comprehend a nutrition and exercise plan.) By this measure, most people can comprehend a well-done financial plan. You are not stupid.

Chapter 7 provides more detail on how the media use our natural emotional biases to nudge us into consumption and financial product decisions, and what we can do to defend against those tendencies.

Flashpoints

It turns out there are specific life situations, or "flashpoints," that turn money messages into our innate personal beliefs about money. Reviewing these situations with an adult eye often helps bring clarity to healthy and unhealthy money messages that reflect—and reinforce—healthy and unhealthy money habits.

In their book, **Mind Over Money**, Ted Klontz, Ph.D., and Brad Klontz, PsyD., CFP® (father and son) discuss these flashpoints and describe how money imbalances and disorders arise. Some financial flashpoints are quite beneficial and teach us positive money behaviors and attitudes. Some may be traumatic, such as being evicted from your home when you are very young. Depending on the messages you've heard around you, a painful and frightening experience like eviction might lead you to worry constantly about financial catastrophe, or to form a rebellious attitude toward money. It may also drive you into becoming a successful saver as a defense mechanism.

Over time, healthy money habits allow us to make rational decisions in our long-term best interests, while unhealthy money habits end up meeting an emotional need. Without realizing it, many of us continue these habits into our adulthood, even if they no longer make any practical sense.

Habits

Few people have perfect balance in their money habits. Most of us veer across a spectrum from good balance to not-so-good balance in our relationship with money. Here are some of the healthy and unhealthy sides to money habits:

Saving Habits

Saving habits are generally terrific, healthy money habits to have. Preparing better for our financial futures seems to be something most Americans would do well to add to their financial behaviors. Saving is a healthy money habit to have for achieving long-term goals like paying for college, buying a home, or entering retirement.

Saving can become imbalanced, however, when saving habits originate from a sense of insecurity, from either fear of future catastrophe or insecurity about self-worth when it's connected to a perceived deficiency in net worth. When saving habits become attempts to feel more secure, we find we never have enough. This kind of saving can deprive us and those around us of simple pleasures, and can cause unhappiness.

Spending on Image Habits

Money allows us to project our self-image: in our dress, dwelling, transportation, health care, and almost any other area of our lives. It is important to make a good impression. However, when we don't have our own self-approval, and we spend to gain others' approval instead, we develop an unhealthy habit tied to an emotional need.

Spending for Fun Habits

Money allows us leisure and time for spontaneity. Planning for every penny ahead of time is not the message of this book. We should occasionally spend our money on unplanned frivolity, and enjoy it.

Young people are notorious for overspending on fun. This is a habit most of us outgrow, but not everyone does. Using money for fun in financially healthy proportions is a tough balancing act, but it's part of becoming more mature and more mindful.

Sharing Habits

Money allows us to feel good by helping others. As you'll read throughout this book, once we have our needs, comforts, and luxuries met, sharing what we have is the surest way to stay happy.

Unhealthy sharing habits appear when we share with expectations attached, or share too freely to our own detriment. Just as with spontaneity, there is a healthy proportion of sharing we can (and should) incorporate into our money mentality.

Money Freedom Habits

One healthy money habit is managing not to think about money at all! When we can spend the right proportion of time free of money thoughts, we have acquired mindful money mentality nirvana.

Yet most of us know people who ignore or deny money's importance. Money comes in and out of their financial lives without discipline, planning, or direction. Also, believing that you are simply "not good with money" can reinforce an already chaotic financial picture. These money beliefs take freedom from money concerns a little too far.

Some unhealthy money habits are so destructive that they qualify as disorders, such as pathological gambling, or extreme financial hoarding. See the Resources in the back of this book if you think you or someone you know might have such a disorder.

Having thought about your own messages, beliefs, and flashpoints, consider the following self-assessment and see if any of its items describe your own habits.

Self-Assessment

What is my earliest memory of learning something about money? _____

_____

_____

_____

_____

_____

What messages about money do I remember from my mother? my father? other authority figures in my family? _____

_____

_____

_____

_____

_____

(Read again the list of money messages in the "Beliefs" section near the beginning of this chapter.)

Which of them, if any, would I add to my list above? _____

_____

_____

Do I see any patterns in my list? What common values appear, if any?

_____

_____

_____

Did I ever rebel against any of these messages? How did I feel before and after that happened? _____

_____

_____

_____

Go back to the list and look at the messages I did not choose. Is there a pattern in them? Is there a common value or values? _____

_____

_____

If I were to describe my internalized money messages to a financial professional, how would I summarize them? _____

_____

_____

_____

Congratulations! You've taken your first step to a mindful money mentality by becoming aware of your money messages. Next we will learn how they influence decisions about spending, saving, sharing, and investing.

(See the Resources and Reading list in the back of this book for more resources on exploring money messages.)

Notes:

1. Pages 14-17: Beliefs and messages adapted from Brad Klontz, Psy. D., and Ted Klontz, Ph.D., **Mind Over Money: Overcoming the money disorders that threaten our financial health**, (New York: Crown Business, 2009) and Syble Solomon, **Money Habitudes: A guide for professionals working with money related issues** (Wilmington, NC: LifeWise Productions, 2009).

Integrating the Money Principles

"It is the chiefest point of happiness that a man is willing to be what he is." ~Desiderius Erasmus

The next step in a mindful approach to money will be to integrate what you've discovered about your past messages and beliefs with your present personal values and principles. Here are some thoughts to consider on principles for saving, spending, sharing, and investing.

Saving: What Is Enough?

It seems to be a given that Americans don't save enough. But only one side of the "enough" equation is explored in public—"enough" being the sum total expressed these days as a "Number." On the other side of the equation are the hard questions that require individual introspection and sometimes assistance from a professional financial planner. If we focus only on "the Number," we are left with the perpetual sense that we are behind, falling short, and thus jeopardizing our future. And anyway, what incentives are being offered—by the media and the financial industry—to make you believe otherwise? Fear is indeed a powerful sales tool.

I have met many people who have saved what turns out to be more than "enough" based on their simple goals for financial independence. The dilemma in their stories, however, is that they often deprive themselves, their children, and their communities of their ample resources because of unwarranted insecurity.

While running out of money in our 80s or 90s should be a bigger concern than dying with too much in the bank, both of these outcomes are based on a common misunderstanding of the meaning of "enough." Anyone who lives with the concept of "I'll never have enough," will suffer. Constantly thinking, "I'll never have enough," has negative mental and physical health effects, which can shorten our lives (which, as noted earlier, is one way to make sure you do have enough, but I don't recommend it).

A Tradeoff Story

An awareness of tradeoffs was my catalyst for leaving corporate America. I entered the banking industry at 20 as a commercial credit trainee and left when I was 40 as a senior vice president in private banking. Throughout my career, I found I enjoyed being a client advocate.

I thought that if I did my best to listen and understand clients' concerns, and if I provided solutions with their best interests in mind, they would remain clients. By doing what was right for them, I was acting in the best interests of the three of us: the bank (which engaged the client), the client (who got what he or she needed), and me (who did the job and got rewarded appropriately for it). For a long time, I worked in an environment where this arrangement seemed to hold true.

After the bank merged with another institution, however, new policies were written. First we as senior account managers had to work with new rules about account size. If certain clients' accounts fell below a minimum level within a specified period of time, I was required to refer those clients to someone else in the organization for service.

We were also required to sell a certain number and variety of financial products, such as insurance, investments, deposits, and loans, to keep the clients and to keep our jobs. It no longer felt like the clients' best interests were coming first.

By 2005, I had decided to jump ship and had formed a business plan to operate as an independent consultant.

Over the next five years, my financial independence came through saving and spending wisely, and by making tradeoffs, like moving from a big house in the city to a small house in the country. Without debt, I found I could work as much or as little as I wanted. While my savings and investments today will clearly not put me in the Forbes 400 or even 400,000, I know my likelihood of running out of money is small.

Having the freedom to spend my time where and how I wish was a higher priority than having a bigger investment account, a bigger house, and an unsatisfying job. By some, but not all, measures I have "a lot," but, more importantly, by my own measure, I have "enough."

The only way you can know whether you'll have "enough" is to define your goals. The first step to doing this is to try and answer a deceptively simple question: What makes you happy?

Discovering the answer may be the biggest contribution you can make to your own well-being and to a spending and saving plan that meshes easily with your goals and values.

Spending: Heartfelt Desire Versus the Wanting Mind

Consumption Default

When we think about money problems, the question of whether we are overspending inevitably arises. In our consumption-driven culture, the answer is often yes, we're overspending. If you have tendencies toward spending, you know that our society easily enables these and even strengthens them. If you do not overspend, you will still wage a constant battle against those spending messages; we all do. (When was the last time you saw an advertisement saying, "Buy less stuff"?)

Buying things can be a convenient way to try to meet emotional needs. Rather than facing our emotions head-on and working through them, we are taught to drown them, numb them, and deny them through purchases. Spending money to feel better becomes an automatic default.

At a low point in my life, I myself went into consumption default mode. I was grieving my father's sudden death when a psychiatrist friend called to check on me. I asked him if there was just one thing, other than a pill, that could help me begin to feel better. I was thinking about a trip to a spa, an appointment with a therapist, or a book. But my real (and silent) question was, "What do I need to buy to make the pain go away?"

My friend's response should not have surprised to me. He said, "I know you may not feel like it, but one of the best antidotes for grief is exercise." "Well," I begrudged, "exercise is not conveniently done from the comfort of my couch," which was where I wanted to stay 24 hours a day for the foreseeable future.

Because I trusted him, I went for a walk around the block that evening. Apathetically trudging through my neighborhood, often in tears, I learned like a reluctant five-year-old that he was right. I did it the next evening, too, and the next, and the next. I did not want to. I just knew I had to.

Those walks cost me nothing. In my anguish, I had been willing to fork over a few hundred dollars to temporarily feel better with massages or pedicures. But in reality, the walking did far more for me than anything I could have bought. I didn't have to spend a nickel to get relief.

How We Spend

Some of us think we "can't afford" to save for retirement, but still choose to spend $2.79 for coffee three times a week. It's like when we grab a brownie when we know we need to lose weight. Short-term rewards can be quite enticing. Consider the following:

Which would you prefer, A or B?

> A. $100 today.

> B. $101 in one week.

What about this offer?

> A. $100 in 52 weeks.

> B. $101 in 53 weeks.

In both cases your reward improves $1 by waiting a week. You made that $1 by waiting on $100, for a return of 1%. That 1% is gained in a week, so if you choose A in either example, you are giving up a 52% annualized (non-compounded) return.

Still, some people will choose A in the first offer but B in the second. If this is you, then you value short-term rewards highly, even though you probably know perfectly well you should be more patient.

The mathematical side of our brain disproportionately values rewards today (spending) over rewards tomorrow (saving). Although that side is rational and smart, when it comes to projecting into the future, it doesn't help us block the emotion attached to the future's uncertainty. So we unconsciously place greater value on the certainty of the present (brownie today - yum) and, due purely to its uncertainty, ignore the future (maybe I will be overweight, but maybe I won't).

When we expect spending to satisfy an emotional need like being popular, having status, or increasing self-esteem, we invariably end up disappointed. This makes us want even more, and more, which will never be enough. We develop what many Buddhist traditions call a "wanting mind."

With a wanting mind, our wants stand in front of us like a rainbow. When you were young, did you ever try to touch a rainbow? The closer you got, the further away it seemed. With a wanting mind, you can spend your life pursuing a rainbow of empty wants, perpetually longing for, rather than finding, the path of lasting satisfaction. Wants and wishes that originate from a place of balance, self-understanding, and self-confidence could be called "heartfelt desires."

What if you want an expensive car, but you are not sure whether it is a heartfelt desire or a symptom of the wanting mind? How do you know the difference?

Distinguishing Heartfelt Desire from the Wanting Mind

Heartfelt desires are long-lasting, imbued with a sense that they are worth waiting for. Wanting-mind desires have unnecessary urgency. Heartfelt desires are more likely to include benefits for others besides ourselves. Wanting-mind desires are typically not achievable without great sacrifice in more important areas. Heartfelt desires are within the realm of long-term possibility while other priorities are kept straight and in sight. Because a wanting mind is never satisfied, its desires are insatiable and often renewed by every interaction with certain people or in certain environments. Heartfelt desires are independent of others' expectations or perceptions. They originate from a strong sense of who we are and a yearning to grow into our purest potential, our happiest self, by fulfilling them.

Former neighbors of mine had a simple rule for figuring out whether a want came from the mind or the heart. Whenever they thought they wanted something big, they would wait 30 days to see if it remained on their minds. This gave the emotion of the moment time to either steep into satisfaction, or disappear altogether. If the emotion was born of unnecessary urgency, waiting gave my friends the time to recognize it as a want that would feel good only temporarily and that would require more later. This rule was a good first defense against impulsive spending on unnecessary wants.

Make the focus of your financial plan the desires of your heart, rather than the objects of a wanting mind.

Sharing Principles: The Happiness Factors

In 2002, the Nobel Prize in Economics was not awarded to an economist. It was awarded to two psychologists, Dr. Daniel Kahneman and (posthumously) Dr. Amos Tversky. Their research focused on measuring how much intangible benefit, or "utility," we derive from things we spend money on.

Let's assume that for $199, I can buy an iPod. To a cost accountant, I have acquired a hunk of metal, plastic, and wires. To an economist, my iPod is a bundle of utility, defined by the pleasure I receive from its ability to download, play, and store customized lists of songs and videos. To me, that bundle of utility is worth $199. But how many "units" of utility did I get with it? To my cousin, it may only be worth

$149, because she derives less utility from the iPod. Therefore, she will not buy an iPod unless the price falls to $149. Note that this is different from thinking she "cannot afford" $199 but "can afford" $149. The price difference merely reflects a difference between two buyers over perceived usefulness (utility), value, or entertainment.

One aspect of utility is happiness. Over time, economists have become interested in how to measure happiness. If happiness could be quantified, then companies could have a better idea of how to price their products and how many of them to produce. You may not be surprised to know that economists have found that happiness is not correlated with how much stuff we have, or even with how much money we have. It is highly correlated with how much time we have, who we regularly spend time with, and how we spend our time.

Many Westerners who travel to developing countries, and get to know the people there, come back with the observation that, "They don't have much, but they sure seem happy anyway." In many countries, people spend time in their own communities and with their own families. Their happiness is defined and ensured by the quality of their personal relationships. News flash: so is ours!

What are the links between financial issues, wealth, and happiness? Some of the results of happiness economics studies may surprise you.

For example, wealthier nations are not necessarily happier than poorer ones. Dr. Robert Biswas-Diener, the "Indiana Jones of Positive Psychology," studied happiness in the slums of Kolkata, India. He looked at happiness in health, self-image, morals, income, looks, and resources, and compared these with their counterparts in America. Kolkatians were found to be happier than Americans in terms of self-image, morals, and looks; but unhappier, unsurprisingly, with their health, income, and resources. Kolkatians also found happiness from their communities far more readily than Americans. They derived more happiness from their close connections to those around them when compared with Americans and their relative isolation from their neighbors.

Most Americans have their basic needs met, something that two billion people in the world do not have: a full stomach, sturdy shoes, warm clothes, and shelter that does not leak. We are literate. We have sports, music, arts, and outdoor leisure opportunities. We have many material reasons to be happy and feel fulfilled. So where is the disconnect?

Money and Fulfillment

What is the relationship between money and fulfillment? As our money increases, does our fulfillment increase at the same rate?

At fairly low levels, a little money buys a lot of fulfillment. When we are young, poor, or hungry, a little money might buy us a hot meal, our first car, our first apartment, or a second-hand coat. That hot meal may not cost much, but the fulfillment gained from it is significant. Do you remember your first car or your first apartment? How fulfilling was it when you first experienced freedom and independence? On a cold day, how much is the basic warmth of a coat worth? At survival levels, the relationship between money spent and fulfillment gained is close, and positive.

Later, when we become fortunate enough to take food, shelter, transportation, and warmth for granted, we use money to buy comforts, or "wants." New furniture. A new coat. A newer car. We still get fulfillment from this money spent, although it's not the same jolt we got from buying the basic survival items.

After we are comfortable, we begin to think about upgrades. A nicer car. A nicer coat. A nicer home in the nicest neighborhood. We treat ourselves to luxuries, or "wishes." Luxuries and wishes also give us a sense of fulfillment, of accomplishment, but again, not the same as with those first survival items, and even less than with comforts and "wants." Economists call this the "diminishing marginal return" of fulfillment.

With each additional dollar we spend throughout our lives, we learn that we gain additional fulfillment, even though the gains are getting smaller. What do many of us do next? We keep spending the dollars and expecting more fulfillment. Some of us acquire bank and investment accounts. Others acquire status. Others acquire stuff.

Eventually the accounts, status, and stuff cease to be comforts or luxuries. They become burdens to acquire, learn, operate, store, protect, finance, upgrade, maintain, and even sell. At that point, they become clutter. They do not add to our fulfillment; they subtract from it.

Yet, even though we know that each additional dollar brings a diminishing unit of happiness, it can be tempting to think, "If I had more money, I could do or have that," or simply, "I would be happier if I had more money." Sometimes even people with little to no debt and a healthy earnings stream think this way.

So how can we extract the most fulfillment from our money before our acquisitions become clutter? By spending it freely, without expectations, on others. That is called "sharing," and, rather than diminishing marginal returns, it produces leaps in happiness with each additional dollar spent.

Understanding how you want to live the next chapter of your life is a worthwhile "end" to have in mind. With a plan and a system, money can help us reach that end, but it is not the answer to our problems or our unhappiness: we are.

It might sound trite, but once we figure out what makes us happy, it is not hard to let other stuff go.

Investing Principles: Optimizers and Satisficers

Biswas-Diener's conclusion from his happiness studies: "Building wealth is important for your happiness, but focusing on it is not."

One general fact of investing is that investments behave randomly. Therefore, they require dealing with uncertainty. We can approach uncertainty in life by one of two ways: as an "optimizer" or a "satisficer." Optimizers constantly strive for more. Satisficers recognize that pursuing more has costs, and stop at "enough."

Optimizers live on a treadmill of constant improvement. In spending, they seek higher and higher levels of sophistication. Yet, as their incomes increase, they also see more and more flaws in their environments .The beer is not quite cold enough. The restaurant table is too close to the kitchen. The hotel room is too far from the elevator. Traveling optimizers have optimized schedules: gym time, breakfast, appointments, dinner, and prearranged show tickets. Optimizers want the fastest route to the destination, because the journey is incidental. Attempting to control the future, rather than living in the now, they are rarely satisfied.

In investing, optimizers want to pick the best mutual fund, the best money manager, or the best bank. Often the "best" to an optimizer means finding the person, or the investment, or the choice that will do the most for the least. Ironically, in this case, increasing income is widely expected to provide more freedom; but as optimizers gain wealth, they hamstring themselves with optimized spending and investing decisions.

Optimizing does not accommodate random events like a flat tire, a sick child, or a market hiccup. Such inconveniences can cause disproportionate stress in the optimizer's life.

On the other hand, satisficers are happier people than optimizers. They know when they have enough. Their goals and desires do not increase lockstep with their achievement of them. Randomness produces uncertainty, but satisficers use uncertainty to contribute to happiness, instead of letting it be a detractor.

Can randomness contribute to happiness? To use a European trip example, satisficers might take the slow train in Italy with the students and retirees, enjoying the scenery, and stopping in random towns. When a satisficer opens his account statement, he already knows he has enough to achieve his goals, so results may be "interesting," but don't make or break his day.

A satisficer with a vague schedule, flexible itinerary, and liberal tastes is like the tennis star waiting for the next serve. Knees and elbows bent, but not rigid, he or she can adroitly handle the ball. Occasionally an ace will fly by, but the satisficer knows that this is something over which she has no control. An optimizer, meanwhile, might throw her racket over the net.

Approaching investing like a satisficer can require great discipline, but is well worth it. In Chapter 7 we will explore the ways we naturally tend toward optimizing rather than satisficing. Whatever resources you need to stay in a satisficing frame of mind, find them, and you will be far happier. (Also see the Resources and Reading list in the back of the book.)

In the next chapter you'll have the chance to apply your saving, spending, and investing principles in several specific areas of your life. The following self-assessment will help you be prepared for some of those areas.

Self-Assessment

What kind of life will I have lived in order to feel satisfied that I was successful? _____

_____

_____

_____

Is my definition of success derived from a heartfelt desire for what truly makes me happy? _____

_____

_____

_____

Have there been times when my definition of success was driven by emotional needs and/or a wanting mind? What was the result? _____

_____

_____

_____

If I could tell a financial professional what "enough" means to me, what would I say? _____

_____

_____

_____

4

Applying Mindfulness in Practice

"Life can only be understood backwards, but it must be lived forwards."
~Soren Kierkegaard

Savings Decisions

College or Retirement?

I am often asked which is more important: saving for retirement, or saving for a child's or grandchild's college education? If I were to decide between the two, I'd choose retirement.

If you are a promising, hard-working, intelligent (and persistent) 17-year-old, there are many programs and options available to help you pay for a college education. There are grants, scholarships from colleges and universities, scholarships from local Rotary clubs and foundations, athletic scholarships, and loans (as a last resort), just to name a few. Our society is geared toward helping you maximize your potential. If you cannot come up with enough personal funds to attend your first-choice university, and you do not want to take out a loan, you have second, third, and fourth choices to explore.

If you are a promising, hard-working, intelligent and persistent 59 1/2-year-old, by comparison, there aren't nearly as many programs and options available to help you have a safe and secure retirement. Our society is not geared, or especially sympathetic, to those who, whether through choice or not, have not saved enough regardless of how bright or promising they are.

So this might not sound like the standard American way, but it is important to make sure Mom and Dad's retirement is on track before saving for a child's college education. If this sounds like the opposite of what most parents do today, well... it is!

A College Decision Tradeoff

Clarence and Ida had two grandchildren. When it came to saving for their grandchildren's college educations, they decided they wanted to put aside enough to enable both of their grandkids to go to any Ivy League school they chose. It sounded like a very worthy goal. But a couple of things about it struck me as odd.

First, the amount of money that would need to be set aside to meet this goal—relative to the couple's resources—was significant. As their financial adviser, I wanted to make sure they understood it clearly before making the commitment.

Second, Clarence had mentioned putting himself through college and having a hard time of it. Perhaps there was an emotional need interfering in their decision.

Third, there were the additional costs of college on top of tuition: living expenses like rent, meals out, transportation to and from home if the college is distant, equipment and supplies, and so on. Had they considered these, and did they really mean they wanted to cover the whole kit-and-kaboodle as a free ride? Or was the goal really more aspirational than realistic?

I asked Clarence to tell me more about putting himself through school. He elaborated on how difficult it had been for him and, because of having to work, he had missed much of the college experience. Remembering this, he had financially helped his own son through public university but now he wanted his grandchildren to have no financial limits on where they went to college and no financial struggles once they arrived.

"That's a very worthy goal," I told him. "But when you say no boundaries, do you mean you want to cover only tuition, books, and board at a private school, or will you also cover computers, apartment rents, fraternity and sorority dues, pizza and beer, flights home, and other such additional costs?"

Suddenly the fantasy began dissolving and reality intruded! Both grandparents looked as if they had not thought of these other expenses. I suggested we look at the range of possible expenditures to see what effect they might have on the original plan. They agreed.

We found that their ability to have sufficient income to maintain their present lifestyle, along with travel, a second home, long-term care insurance, and dining out three times a week would clearly be affected by saving for a Harvard education versus an education at a public university. In saving for a Harvard education for two grandchildren, they faced a 70% probability of continuing to live the life they wanted. This was certainly not terrible, but if they chose instead to save for a public university education for two, then that probability went to 95%. Clearly much better.

I didn't like giving them the news that they might not be best served by promising their grandchildren an all-expenses-paid Ivy League education. But I did say: "This seems pretty important to you. Are you sure you want to make the adjustments needed in your own lives that would allow you to achieve this one?"

Ida spoke up first: "Absolutely not! I want them to have a good college education, but I want to have my life, too." Clarence agreed: "Yes, it would have been nice, but wow, I didn't realize it would require that much." In the end they decided to put funds aside for two public university educations—tuition, room, and board only.

Below are some questions and details to explore about saving for college for a child or grandchild.

Self-Assessment: Saving for College

Acceptable level of college support I could provide: _____

_____

_____

Ideal level of college support I could provide: _____

_____

_____

Year(s) in which kids/grandkids will be starting college: _____

_____

Number of years of college attendance I plan to support: _____

_____

Will I support living expenses, as well as school expenses? If so, to what extent? What expenses will be considered "off-limits"? _____

_____

_____

Retirement: More Than A Number

For a while it was fashionable to ask, "What's my Number?" to establish an ideal figure for retirement. But as a one-dimensional question, it implied that there would be a simple, one-dimensional answer. In fact, "What's my Number?" left little room for anything other than one-dimensional assumptions about inflation, taxes, IRA rules, income, expenses, and interest rates. And it left no room for a possible lifestyle somewhere on the spectrum between Lifelong Ideal and Minimum Comfort. "What's my Number?" really doesn't consider you as an individual with a unique life ahead of you. No wonder the fruitless attempt to answer it causes so much anxiety and gets so much press.

> *"Would you tell me, please, which way I ought to go from here?"*
> *"That depends a good deal on where you want to get to," said the Cat.*
> *"I don't much care where..." said Alice.*
> *"Then it doesn't matter which way you go," said the Cat.*
> *"... so long as I get SOMEWHERE," Alice added as an explanation.*
> *"Oh, you're sure to do that," said the Cat, "if you only walk long enough."*
> *(Alice's Adventures in Wonderland, Chapter 6)*

Money must have a direction, just like a car. The direction you point it in depends on where you want to go—your ideal destination. Most online financial tools, for example, assume that we all want the same destination: a flat annual retirement income figure. That one figure is supposed to provide the security that ensures that we'll have enough to fulfill all of our needs, wants, and wishes.

But clearly, we *all* have more than just one "Number," and the number will differ from person to person. Some "numbers" recur every month. Some come in chunks every few years. Others won't be due until a distant future date but can then become a twice-yearly expense.

Telling our money to provide a flat annual income to meet other-than-annual expenses is like having a car that will only take you to the grocery store but nowhere else.

A Range Versus A Number

Clarence and Ida's story vividly illustrates the benefit of using a range of variables to make savings decisions rather than using a single number. Did you notice how their college funding goal was finally altered to accommodate their lifestyle goals? In order to make a mindful decision about college savings, they needed to make sure their other savings goals were going to be met as well.

By considering a range of needs rather than a single number, Clarence and Ida made the tradeoff decision more comfortably. When defining the high end of a goal's range, the "ideal" amount would be the number you'd most like to have in order to both offer a generous gift—like an education—and maintain your preferred lifestyle. In their case, this "ideal" included an all-expenses-paid Ivy League education for two grandchildren plus their own lifestyle comfort in later life. At the other end of the range, the "acceptable" amount would be the number that represents still "good enough." For Clarence and Ida, the choice meant a public university education with no extra paid expenses.

The turning point for Clarence and Ida came when they saw how their spending on college would affect their other lifestyle retirement goals. It included a consideration of the calculated chance that they would outlive their money. With the "ideal" college savings plan, they started with a 30% chance (70% success rate = 30% failure rate) and by adjusting their goal to the "acceptable," they decreased that chance to 5%. (By the way, there is no way, theoretically, to reduce the chance of outliving your money to zero. Avoid anyone who makes you this promise!)

If you get stuck, try to imagine the experiences you are likely to have with your "ideal" plan and your "acceptable" plan, and decide which one is more personally lasting and meaningful.

Where Do You Want Your Money To Take You?

If you get behind the wheel of a car, turn on the ignition, put it in gear, but don't have any idea where you want to go, who's in charge? You, or the vehicle? Driving a car without a destination is downright dangerous. Buying financial products without defining your goals is just as dangerous. Yet both professionals and clients can lose touch with that idea and end up chasing products down dead-end roads.

What are the possible places you might want to "drive" to? Consider the list of "unsatisfactory" and "satisfactory" destinations below.

Unsatisfactory destinations:

- Rich Land. (Most of us are already there, by comparison with much of the rest of the world.)
- Maximum Growth and No Risk Land. (Is there any such place, really?)
- 100% Guaranteed Income Land (In your dreams!)
- Cake-and-Eat-It-Too Land (Easy enough to love!)
- Whatever-the-Most-My-Portfolio-Can-Make-Me Land (without any consideration of those variables we discussed earlier)
- Best-of-Everything Land (Who has that?)

Many of these destinations really only exist in Fantasy Land; they are too vague for any kind of meaningful roadmap. After a while, heading for one of these destinations, a driver would be exhausted, and at the mercy of the vehicle, and would not be getting to the preferred destination anyway.

Satisfactory destinations:

- The land of replacing the car with one like it every five years until I can't drive anymore.
- The land of spending three weeks every year in Scotland beginning in two years.
- The land of putting my kids (or grandkids) through private school.
- The land of buying a mountain house by the time I'm 65.
- The land of hosting my children and/or grandchildren on a cruise every summer beginning next year.
- The land of building my own boat in two years.
- The land of establishing a permanent endowment at the university music school in one year.
- The land of hosting a 50th anniversary party for my parents.
- The land of going to graduate school full-time in two years.
- The land of spending 20 hours per week volunteering at the homeless shelter beginning next year.

I didn't have to make these up. They are real destinations, courtesy of real clients. Some of these destinations people knew right off the bat. Others took some time to discover.

Figuring out your own destinations can be hard work. But once you know them, you can establish what you need to get there—what kind of vehicle you'll need, whether it should have snow tires, four-wheel drive, a sunroof, manual transmission, tinted windows, or halogen headlights. The answers to your questions about how to get there will start to fall into place.

If your goal is to lead a happy, fulfilling life without running low on money, then you need to examine how your goals, and the ways you'll achieve them, will affect your life over the long term.

A Spending/Saving Scenario to Consider

Wonderful news. Your plan shows that the odds are 99% that you can make the ideal version of your spending plan work for the rest of your life, with no worries about running out of money.

But before you pop the champagne cork, let's examine your plan again.

Did you include every need, want, and wish that has crossed your mind? Maybe you left out a second home, or a gift to your alma mater, in order to be conservative. That's okay, but what if you reduced your ideal goal toward the acceptable level and could add one of the wishes you excluded before? What if you could buy the second home, but would be replacing your car every seven years instead of every four? Would you want to make those tradeoffs?

Or, would the satisfaction of endowing a college scholarship outweigh the enjoyment of an extra 3000 square feet of living space?

What if, on the other hand, your plan shows that you don't have enough to ensure minimum acceptable goals for the remainder of your life? This could be due to having too much debt, too much spending, or too little savings.

If your problem is too much debt, try consulting with your local not-for-profit credit counseling service. (In some communities, these are agencies funded by the United Way.) Or, if you want to work out your debt without credit counseling, check out Dave Ramsey's website (https://www.daveramsey.com/category/tools/) and look in the library for Ramsey's book, **The Total Money Makeover**. Other resources for increasing savings and decreasing spending can be found in the Resources and Reading List in the back of this book.

If there is a large gap between what you need and what you have, there is no investment strategy that will bridge that gap. Adjusting savings and spending has a far greater effect on long-term financial health than any investment could ever have.

Spending Decisions

Tracking Down the Basics

It helps some people to list their goals for money, prioritizing by needs, wants, and wishes. Abraham Maslow's Hierarchy of Needs model says that the first human needs that must be met are for physical safety and security. In today's financial planning language, those needs fall into the general categories of shelter (rent or mortgage), maintaining health, and securing food, clothing, transportation, and insurance. These needs must be met at the minimum acceptable level. (Taxes don't feel like needs, but if not met, they can put our other needs in jeopardy, so we have to remember those, too.)

Then, there are other categories, depending upon your plans and resources, such as things like Toys and Travel. These might be called "Wants" or "Wishes."

Wants—the kind worth saving for—are the things that drive us to achieve an extra level of satisfaction, like a new warm coat or a weekend getaway.

Wishes are the things we dream about. While realistic and attainable, they may seem part of a distant future, like a boat, an antique, or an additional home. Achieving wishes brings even stronger feelings of freedom and self-development.

One way to get an idea of how much you need for basic safety and security is to track what you presently spend on them. Even if you think you overspend, having a starting number based upon reality is better than relying on a guess. Sometimes, careful tracking is all that is needed to ensure that spending habits reflect a healthy relationship with money.

There are many ways to track living expenses, depending on what suits you. At a minimum, you'll need checkbooks, online banking records, credit card statements, and any other records of the ways you spend money.

Getting the basic living expenses wrong can derail your success. If you simply guess at them, without using good records, and you guess too low, you increase your chances of living in a state of perpetual insecurity. If you are conservative and you guess high, you could make decisions that can deprive you of your dreams, wishes, or other sources of happiness, and that can bring big regrets later.

If you have never done this exercise before, record for one to three months what you spend on the following:

- Groceries
- Clothing
- Shoes
- Medications
- Doctor visits
- Dentist visits
- Eyeglasses or contacts
- Gas and repairs for the car
- Car insurance
- Gym membership or exercise class dues
- Health insurance

- Disability insurance
- Income taxes
- Property taxes

Once you have collected this information, then inflate those dollars over time. Inflation of 3% a year might not sound like much, but when you compound 3% over many years, it adds up significantly. Your monthly budget for groceries today might only buy you lunch later in life. (As an example, look what a postage stamp cost when you were 20. How much is it today? Project that difference between now and the time you are 80. If a postage stamp costs $1.50 by then, what will also happen to the price of clothes? food? shelter?) Inflation may wax and wane, but over a couple of decades, its effect on our spending can be significant, and vital to consider.

If you do not have a good idea of your basic living expenses, and are not comfortable with tracking them, or with calculating inflation and compounding calculations, then hire an hourly financial planner or personal daily money manager to help you with this task. (Again refer to the Resources and Reading List.)

Shelter (your home)

Shelter, along with its attending property taxes, insurance, association dues, repairs and upkeep, and mortgage payments (or rent), is normally the largest of our basic living expenses. Is your current home going to suffice to provide the kind of life you want, at any level? Or, what kind of home would be enough to provide the life you want? Let's examine this question.

What Kind of Home?

One of the first questions many real estate agents ask a buyer is, "How much home can you afford?" They should probably be asking instead: "What kind of home are you looking for?"

Adapted from the book by John E. Nelson and Richard Bolles, **What Color Is Your Parachute? For Retirement,** homes can generally fall into one or a combination of five possible uses:

1. As a jobsite: For some people, working on their home is an enjoyable avocation. Building a deck, expanding the master bedroom, transforming a child's room into a study or other projects can keep them happily occupied. Having a home with something to improve upon gives them meaning.

2. As a gallery or museum: For some, a home is a place to display, for themselves and/or for others. The display may be of art, furniture, collectibles, knick-knacks, cars, antique tractors, or Harleys. Not to be confused with hoarding, this kind of "collecting" provides long-lasting personal meaning. It can strengthen ties with like-minded groups or aficionados. It can bring great satisfaction and happiness to have a place in which to cultivate, display, and admire objects.

3. As community center: Home for some people is a gathering place. Having family and friends visiting regularly is a source of pleasure, not a burden. Home for them brings the enjoyment of having company and sharing their space with others.

4. As a base of operations: On-the-go people use a home mostly as a rest stop. It may be a place to exchange one suitcase for another.

5. As a retreat: The opposite of the home-as-community-center, home for some people is a private sanctuary. It is the place where they recharge.

How Many Homes?

Are you considering a second home? Becoming a "snowbird" or having a country place and a city place? Might your second home be in a resort community, a community near a college or university, or in an active outdoor setting? Happiness for many depends upon being around people who "fill up their tank," and on the small, repeated experiences that give them joy and opportunity. Happiness and health may also depend on having access to healthcare resources that are important to you. Make sure, if you decide on a second home, that you have enough access to the people and resources you want and need to live happily and healthfully.

Without careful planning, here's what can happen. Jim thought he wanted to live in the mountains, so he purchased a home in a gated community there. The community had golf, two lakes, a river, and a country club with a nice restaurant. He loved golf and fishing, so it seemed perfect. However, once he got there, he realized that more than two-thirds of the community's homeowners were absentees, like him. Most of the time he was there, the place seemed empty. Compared to his Florida retirement community, it was quiet, but also kind of boring. After two years, he realized the whole purchase was a mistake, and he put it on the market.

Home for the Holidays?

As children become adults and have their own families, grandparents may want to keep their home as a place for family gatherings. Sometimes this preference can even be a contingency plan for an adult child who hasn't quite left the nest and needs more time to do so. Or the home can be a gathering place but only during the holidays.

If you are hanging on to a larger house than you need for the sake of a one- or two-week period every year, try looking at the difference in costs between the larger house and a smaller one you might otherwise choose to live in. Subtract the cost of a downsized house from the cost of your current larger house. Then compare the expenses of maintaining each house year-round, including the taxes, insurance, utilities, and repairs. For the difference in house maintenance costs alone, might it be possible to start a new holiday family-gathering tradition? A cruise? A week at a nice resort? Sometimes it can be hard to let go of the familiar traditions, but having a new one to look forward to can make the transition easier.

If you have a spouse or significant other in your life and find that you do not agree on either keeping or selling a larger house, try reading **What Color Is Your Parachute? For Retirement** (the Nelson and Bolles book) together.

Self-Assessment: What is "Home"?

How is my home used now? _____

_____

_____

How would I like my home, this one or another one, to be used in the future? _____

_____

Primary use of my home: _____

_____

*Secondary use of my home:*_____

_____

What is the minimum space I need in order to live an acceptable lifestyle?

_____

_____

*What is the maximum time and money I want to spend for cleaning and maintaining?*_____

_____

_____

*Should I stay in the geographic area where I am now?*_____

_____

At what point, if any, might it make sense to simplify, or even live abroad?

_____

_____

Annual Costs of Home (complete for each home in question):

*Property Taxes*_____

*Association Dues*_____

*Insurance*_____

*Repairs or Upkeep*_____

*Mortgage or Rent*_____

Health

If we are not healthy, we have a harder time enjoying the people, activities, and groups we love. Lack of health also means that more of our money goes to doctors, prescriptions, and health services than for other important areas of our lives.

Health insurance and/or Medicare premiums should be included in your basic spending, although the choices we make in purchasing health insurance are easy compared to the choices we make to maintain our health. Having a health care (care, not insurance) plan can be as important as a financial plan.

Self-Assessment: My Health Plan

How will I stay healthy and active throughout my life? _____

_____

_____

_____

What activities do I enjoy? _____

_____

_____

_____

Do I belong to a health club? have a personal trainer? walk? golf? play Wii? _____

_____

_____

*What activities would I like to start? stop?*_____

_____

_____

_____

Physical activities to start or continue and their cost(s): _____

_____

_____

_____

What kind of health resources do I need, want, and wish for? (Perhaps you love your general practitioner or your internist and want to stay with him or her. Or, you like to have massages, acupuncture, go to yoga class, or have access to a health food store or a compounding pharmacy.) _____

_____

_____

_____

*What resources do I need that will enable me to take care of my health in ways I'm most comfortable with?*_____

_____

_____

_____

Needs and costs for maintaining my health: _____

_____

_____

Ideal health care resources and their costs: _____

_____

_____

_____

Medical Expenses and Health Savings Accounts

Be sure to keep all of your receipts for medical expenses, including over-the-counter (OTC) medications. Although the limit for deducting expenses is high (at least 10% of your adjusted gross income for most taxpayers), the list of expenses you can include in the calculation is long. Be sure to see the list at the IRS's Publication 502:

http://www.irs.gov/publications/p502/ar02.html#en_US_2012_publink1000178885.

If you do not have high ongoing medical expenses and you have a high-deductible health insurance plan available to you with a health savings account (HSA), take advantage of the HSA. An HSA is an account that allows you to deduct your contribution, and all of the growth in the account is tax-free as well if you take withdrawals for eligible medical expenses. Talk to your accountant; HSAs can often beat IRAs for double tax benefits.

Long-Term Care and End of Life Issues

Many of us do not want to contemplate the time when we will need assistance to care for ourselves, but longer life expectancy brings a greater likelihood of needing long-term care. Medicare and Medicaid cover illness and accidents, but not ongoing daily care. Elderly people who need assistance with two activities of daily living (ADL – such as bathing, toileting, dressing, transferring, eating, and grooming) often rely either on a family member or a professional caregiver if they are not in an assisted living facility. Caring for an elderly person can be stressful and exhausting for family members, but professional alternatives are expensive. Check into long-term care (LTC) insurance if you do not have it already. Resources for evaluating LTC insurance options are listed in the Resources and Reading list.

Food and Groceries

Making mindful choices in the grocery store often puts us at odds with ourselves.

We can eat cheaply but unhealthfully, or we can pay more to eat better. America has become a country where obesity is a disease of the poor. Unfortunately in our food system, cheap food is generally bad for our health, and can promote unhealthy eating habits. Products made from corn, wheat, rice, potatoes, oil, and fatty cuts of beef and pork are ubiquitous. Fresh fruit, fresh vegetables, and lean cuts can be harder to find in some neighborhoods and cost more per calorie. A $2.69 fast-food hamburger goes a long way toward reducing hunger. A $2.69 head of broccoli, unfortunately, will not.

With the advent of grocery warehouses (like Costco and BJ's) selling in bulk, many home pantries and freezers have been turned into mini-warehouses of their own. Sometimes bulk food sits in our own homes until it expires. To be more mindful of food purchases, consider whether bulk buying is in your best interest, health-wise and money-wise.

Self-Assessment: Food and Groceries

How many days of food do I keep on hand at any time? _____

How often do I shop? _____

What do I spend on an average grocery store trip? _____

Do I have an extra refrigerator or freezer, or both, in my home or garage?

_____

What's in that extra refrigerator or freezer? _____

_____

How often do I throw out ruined or spoiled food? _____

_____

What is my grocery spending range? (weekly, monthly, or annually): __

_____

Transportation

Transportation for many people is the second largest spending category. In most of America, except in a few large cities, you need at least one car. The sooner you are able to pay cash for it, the less interest you pay, and the more of your monthly income is available for saving, or needs, wants, and wishes.

The ideal price for your transportation might be $60,000 for your car, while $30,000 would be perfectly acceptable. For city-dwellers, the $30,000 car might be ideal, and a $2,000 annual bus and train budget would be perfectly acceptable.

Cars do not last forever, so just as important as deciding what to spend on a car is deciding how often you plan to replace it.

When thinking about spending and later replacing, consider how much driving you will be doing. What is the distance between people and places—say, between your best friend and your best medical practitioner? Between your favorite grocery store and your favorite park?

Self-Assessment: Transportation/Cars

Priority I give to having a car: _____ (On a scale of 1 to 10, where 10 means you absolutely need a car of any kind, and 1 means you do not need a car at all, but it would be nice to have one.)

Cost of my acceptable car:_____

Cost of my ideal dream car:_____

Year I will need to replace my current car:_____

I would ideally replace my car every _____ years but would accept replacing it every _____ years.

A Note on Leasing

Some people believe that paying cash for cars is fine, unless you can legitimately deduct car lease payments for a business you own. An accounting case can be made for the fact that, if you can deduct the entire lease payment plus operating costs as a business expense, you may get a higher deduction faster than through the conventional depreciation method. However, with Section 179 of the Tax Code, most car purchases are deductible for a business anyway. The non-tax, economic issue with a lease is that you are essentially handing over control of a future decision about your car's value to a large financial entity whose interests are at odds with yours. In the case of a car lease, the leasing company is determining the residual value your car will have at the end of the lease, and using that figure to determine your lease payments. It is in the leasing company's best interests to make that value as low as possible, so that they can make a bigger profit reselling your car when you turn it in. Your payments reflect that bias, so that when you go to make your next lease deal or buy your next car, you may be further behind than you would have been if you traded in, or sold outright, a car you owned.

Clothing

Clothing Supply and Closet Velocity

Clothing is a category in which we all have a lot of discretion. It also highlights the impact many seemingly small discretionary spending decisions can have.

On a visit to Ghana, West Africa, in 2004, I noticed how many people wore second-hand Western clothing. While the country had its own beautiful traditional fabrics and garments, there was also a plethora of screen printed American t-shirts, Gap khakis and Levi's at the local markets. My hosts told me these were *obruni waawu*, which, literally translated, means "dead white people's clothes."

Why dead? I wondered. Before long, an answer dawned. Perhaps to Ghanaians, many of whom don't have closets, the only reason you'd give up perfectly good clothes would be because you are dead. To them, clothes are something you use until they are no longer useable, closets or not.

This led me to wonder just how often we Americans buy new clothes. I had had clients with clothing budgets ranging anywhere from $2,000 to $50,000 a year. But what I had never asked them was how often they were throwing out old clothes.

If we throw out old ones when we buy new ones, I would say we have a "high closet velocity." The amount of clothing we have on hand at any point in time might be called our "clothing supply."

If you have a low clothing supply and low closet velocity, you are like a Ghanaian wearing your small supply of clothes until they wear out and then only replacing them when they have holes or stains. If you have a high clothing supply and high closet velocity, you started with lots of clothes and you're buying more new clothes, but you are also giving or throwing away "old," or more likely, seldom (or never)-worn ones. You might be the Imelda Marcos (the wife of a Filipino president who owned an outlandish number of shoes) of clothes.

If you have a low clothing supply and high closet velocity, you have a small, actively-traded closet. New clothes are entering constantly, but getting worn, and old clothes are going out. You have a high clothing budget, and you always look good. If you have a high clothing supply and low closet velocity, you probably have a large closet of seldom-worn items, with plenty to choose from, although some items might be a bit dated.

Self-Assessment: Clothing

*How much of my monthly income am I spending, and will need to spend, on new clothes? (Imagine the range between ideal and acceptable, and remember that you can make tradeoffs later should you need to.)*_____

_____

Ideal annual spending on clothing: _____

*Acceptable annual spending on clothing:*_____

What kind of closet do I need to store the clothes I actually wear?

*My ideal closet:*_____

*My acceptable closet:*_____

Insurance

It seems the more we have, the more we have to worry about. When we worry about "stuff," and have a lot of "stuff," we tend to want to insure it.

Assume now that you own only the things—possessions—that satisfy your heartfelt desires, and therefore are the things you want to insure. When buying any kind of insurance, compare premiums for the highest and lowest deductibles available. Note the difference, for example, that you'll pay in premiums for a $1000 versus a $5000 deductible (Note you would be risking paying the $4000 difference). If the difference in premiums is $50 per year, you are paying $50 per year to insure against losing $4000. Even though $50 may seem small, it is very high for the extra $4000 risk. You may be paying $2000 to insure a $300,000 house – that's .67% of the amount at risk. Paying $50 to make the deductible $1000 instead of $5000 is an insurance "rate" of 1.25%.

This is an example that may vary significantly from your local rates and premiums. Take the time to do the math and calculate the difference.

As we get older and retire, we may no longer need some kinds of insurance, like life and disability insurance, because we are no longer earning income and our dependents may be financially self-sufficient without life insurance. Instead we may need other kinds, like long-term care insurance and Medicare supplemental/Medigap. In your spending plan, include all insurance premiums that are appropriate for you. Consider these important areas: life, health, dental, disability, long-term care, property (homes, autos, boats, other toys), and umbrella liability. (Umbrella liability is a special kind of liability coverage that is over and above the liability coverage on your individual home and auto policies. It can protect your other assets in case of an accident. When you have your will and estate planning documents drafted or reviewed, ask your attorney for his or her advice on umbrella liability coverage).

With insurance, people who have no cash reserves have fewer choices when it comes to protecting themselves. They need to buy more insurance coverage, with the lowest possible deductibles, because they have no cash through which to self-insure. People who are debt-free, with savings and investments, have more insurance choices. They can make informed decisions about what risks they are willing to take themselves and which ones they choose to offload to an insurance company.

Once you are debt-free and begin to accumulate healthy savings and investments, consider where you really "need" insurance and where you might be able to self-insure. For instance, could you keep fire and liability coverage on your country cabin, but drop flood insurance? This does not mean you believe it won't flood. It only means that you are willing to take on this risk yourself, because you believe it is small.

When offered one-time insurance on something like a potential airplane accident, consider the cost in light of the true probability of the insurable event. With commercial flights, for example, your odds of being in an accident are 1 in 29 million. If your life is worth $5 million (in terms of lost expected lifetime earnings), then theoretically, a reasonable insurance premium for one flight segment is 1/29 million x $5 million, or about 17 cents. If you fly ten segments a year, that would be $1.70 annually. Check this against the cost of flight insurance for just one flight segment! (You can look up probabilities of remote events on Google or Ask.com. Be sure to check the sources of the statistics to see if they are credible.)

Self-Assessment: Insurance

Is there anything I am insuring that I don't need or can't replace? _____

Is there anything I could self-insure? _____

Have I examined the difference in premium between low and high deductibles? _____

Spending Decisions: Wants and Wishes

Toys

Could some kinds of "toys" be considered "needs," not simply wants or wishes? When you are 95 and want to have no regrets, what toys would you have wanted to enjoy?

When we were married, someone gave my husband a button that said "He who dies with the most toys wins." Moving into our first apartment, I was amazed at the number of his toys. The extra closet was not for my clothes and shoes, but for his wet suit, SCUBA tanks, bow and arrows, camo clothes, tents, lanterns, and the Coleman stove. Toys!

However, nothing in the "toy closet" went unused. I quickly became SCUBA certified and added my own gear to the collection. We went diving and camping year-round. He went on bird and deer hunts and brought back meat for the freezer. We both loved being outdoors. I felt fortunate that at such a young age, we had clearly identified the activities that brought us great happiness.

For us, nothing in the toy closet was there because we "might use it someday," or because it was 50% off. I think the fact that we were prudent about keeping the collection lean contributed to our satisfaction with our experiences. When a toy became old or broken, we threw it away and decided whether or not a replacement would come into the closet; if there was any chance we wouldn't use it, the replacement could wait, especially if we didn't have cash to buy it. Although we could increasingly afford more expensive toys, we remained vigilant about having just enough for our favorite activities.

The point is not to die with the most toys. The point is to have the toys you desire for a lifetime of experiences with the people and activities that bring you joy.

It is tempting to become overly attached to the things we own that seem useful. Often we hold onto possessions that once gave us comfort or pleasure, but now may merely be clutter, if we looked at them honestly. Clutter creates stress in our lives, more than we may realize, because every time we look at it, we may feel the need to make a decision: keep it or lose it. And "losing," even when it's clutter, feels bad to our emotional brain. So, it is only human and natural to avoid that feeling of loss. But constant decision-making about clutter can be taxing.

Overcoming "clutter loss avoidance" by clearing out the clutter can bring a feeling of great freedom. We need to make fewer keep-or-lose decisions when we no longer serve as the storage space for the clothing, food, and comforts we think we, our family, or our friends might need some day. Note that the places where we buy things are called "stores." Let the stores store it until we are ready to buy it! Let the charities and the incinerator have it when we are through with it.

Keeping our "stuff" supplies and velocities low means less waste in the waste can, less wasted space, less wasted money, more free time, and more emotional freedom, too.

Self-Assessment: Toys

What is my toy closet velocity? _____

_____

*An example of something I threw or gave away when I was truly done with it was...*_____

_____

*How about my toy closet supply? Do I have stuff that no longer satisfies any kind of heartfelt desire?*_____

Travel

Many people want to travel more once they become financially independent. Travel experiences can result in much more remembered happiness than many toys can through ownership. Travel experiences also do not have to be long and/or exotic to bring the same amount of remembered happiness. An eight-day trip to Hawaii is likely to bring about the same fond memories as a 14-day trip. If the choice is between Hawaii and New Zealand, the difference in remembered happiness might only be incremental, particularly if there is no sentimental attachment to one or the other. Additionally, the farther the destination, the more potential for mishaps and travel misery. On the flip side, though, many see the potential for mishaps and misery as an adventurous challenge.

Remember that regret in later life comes more from things we did not do. If there is a place you have been dreaming about visiting for a long time, consider whether there is a way you could visit on a lower budget sooner rather than later. You can always go back a second time on a five-star itinerary if you wish and are able. I have met too many who had a desire to visit a far-off destination, but life events at an older age, whether a bad knee or an ill family member, made the likelihood they would ever make it there smaller and smaller.

With a mindful financial lifestyle plan, your choice about the level and amount of travel, instead of being discarded until "the time is right," should be included. If your Ideal choices turn out to cause too much sacrifice in other areas, perhaps Acceptable choices would not.

Self-Assessment: Travel

If I have a desire to travel, where would I go, how would I travel, how often, and with whom? My desired destination(s) are: (Rank and prioritize these destinations, travel means, and people. If you have trouble, imagine you have 360 days to spend in all of the destinations, and that's it. How many days would you spend in each place?) _____

_____

_____

_____

_____

_____

_____

Does my desire to travel follow one of my hobbies or interests? To see family as often as I would like, is travel required? What are the reasons for my travel to each place? _____

_____

_____

What modes of travel do I prefer? Train, car, Harley Davidson, an RV, bicycle, private plane, transoceanic flight? (For some people, the mode of travel is the object of the trip.) _____

_____

_____

How many trips per year will I take and for how long? _____

_____

_____

Who do I want to travel with? How well do our schedules and personalities mesh? Do I prefer tour groups, my spouse or partner only, children and grandchildren, or a small group of friends? _____

_____

_____

Decisions About Sharing

The Dictator Game and a Charitable Plan

Stephen Dubner, co-author of the best selling book, **Freakonomics**, at a talk in 2012 described a common psychology experiment in which college students are given $3 simply for showing up to participate. Then they are given ten $1 bills and told that another student down the hall was also given $3 but not the $10. The students are then told they are free to share as much or as little of their $10 with the other student as they would like. How much do you think the first students shared on average with the anonymous second student? Answer: $3.

Before giving the audience that answer, however, Dubner asked, "If you were the first student, how much would you share? How many of you would share $10?" Out of 200 people, two hands went up. "Well, there are always a couple of Gandhis in the room," he said. "How many of you would share $5?" Lots of hands. "Three?" A few more hands.

"How many of you would share nothing?" About ten hands went up. "You guys must be the economics students and professors," he said.

In Dubner's experiment, this is how he said trained economists would perceive the situation: "The $10 has been given to ME, so it is MY money, and that student down the hall is NOT ME. So if it is MY money, and he is NOT ME, then that must mean I keep it for ME."

Later Dubner added that most economists want to know that the single student would make the highest and best use of the money before he was given it.

Psychologists call this The Dictator Game because the student who is given the $10 has all the power and all the money. Dubner went on to describe other variations of the game, detailed in **SuperFreakonomics** (another of Dubner's books). The variations showed that the Dictator Game was a flawed indicator of a student's altruism. In fact, a student's altruism would also be influenced by whether or not the student knew that someone was watching the decision he or she made; and by how the giving choice in the question was framed.

Ever been to a charity auction and watched in awe at the prices people pay? Charities know that some altruistic people can be persuaded to give more if their donation is made in public, in a fun and competitive setting, rather than in private and anonymously. Others are the opposite. Knowing and respecting a donor's style of altruism could help charities raise more funds for good causes.

Knowing how certain factors affect our willingness to part with our money can also help us make better decisions, whether we're expecting a request for money or are caught off guard. Make a charitable plan an integral part of your financial plan, and share your intention with the charities that will benefit from your generosity. Sharing your intention is like mortar in a charitable plan: it solidifies your commitment and reduces the chance you will deviate.

Some people have problems saying no to charities. But with a charitable plan in place, when you are approached by a charity not on your list, you can say that you have already made your plan for the coming year (or decade, or lifetime). If you are truly interested in the charity's mission, you could ask it to contact you again when you will be revising your plan. (October-November is a good time for charitable plan review, along with year-end tax planning.)

However, if you are not interested in the charity's mission, you can simply say you've already done your charitable planning. (But, don't say it like a dictator. Instead, pretend you are an economist!)

Many cities and towns have local community foundations to which donations can be made. They do much of the legwork of investigating the administrative efficiency of local charities they represent. For example, if your passion is animal rescue, your local community foundation could tell you how it investigates animal rescue organizations and which of these make the "approved" list. In giving to the community foundation, if anything ever goes wrong at a charitable organization, the community foundation can redirect your donation to a similar charity. Most community foundations are self-supporting and charge little to nothing to administer your funds. But be sure to ask, just in case.

Writing down your charitable plan is another way of making more mindful decisions about sharing. It can help you remember why and for what you are willing to sacrifice other comforts and luxuries. It could also show you that now is the time to enjoy the people or activities that are most important in your life, by sharing with them.

The self-assessment below might help you make decisions about giving to a particular charity. You can also check out many charities at www. charitynavigator.org.

Self-Assessment: Charitable Planning

Can I remember a time when I felt a sense of satisfaction from helping someone else, through donating either time or money? _____

_____

_____

How did that activity connect with something I am passionate about? __

_____

_____

Are there ways I could incorporate more of that kind of activity into my life?

_____

_____

_____

What causes are important to me? (List between two and ten of them here. Then write them as a list in priority order. If you have trouble, imagine that you have $100,000 to split among them. How would you do that?) _____

_____

_____

_____

Estate Planning

Planning your estate is another way of sharing. In documenting how we want our property distributed after our death, we save our heirs and possibly the state from deciding for us. That in itself is a gift.

In most states, if you die without a will, a judge must decide what happens to your assets. Most states have statutes requiring a certain percentage in those cases to go to a spouse and children. In the absence of a will, you cannot assume that everything will automatically go to your spouse or that a judge's decision about distribution of your estate will be made quickly. Some probate courts handle newly filed cases with great efficiency and within a couple of weeks. Others can take months. Meanwhile, all of your family members will be anxiously awaiting the judge's decision and simultaneously grieving for your loss. Spare them the anguish. Get some real legal documents.

In most states there are five basic documents you would be well served to prepare and finalize:

- A will
- A living will
- A durable power of attorney, to handle your financial affairs while you are alive but possibly unable to do so
- A health care power of attorney, to make health care decisions in your behalf in case you are unable to
- A HIPAA designation, telling doctors and hospitals which individuals are allowed to have access to your medical records
- Additionally, in some states, attorneys also prepare a pre-need guardianship document stating whom you would like to name as your guardian in the event of your incapacity.

To properly cover your bases, you may be in good hands when you hire a board-certified estate-planning attorney. Most cities have local estate planning councils to which such professionals belong. Check the National Association of Estate Planning Councils, www.naepc. org. You can also search for and check an attorney's credentials and peer reviews at www.martindale.com.

Most attorneys will provide you with a checklist of questions to answer and an inventory of assets and liabilities to complete. If you do not want to complete the inventory, your financial professional can provide the data most attorneys need.

Distribution decisions are the area where many people get stuck. How will you be able to treat everyone both equally and fairly? Effective professionals, whether legal, tax, or financial, can provide appropriate options to address your concerns.

In addition to leaving property in a will, some people choose to draft ethical wills, which are not legal documents. Ethical wills outline the values, historical perspectives, and hopes that they wish to impart to their loved ones. See the Resources and Reading List for more information on ethical wills.

Once you have made and documented your estate-sharing decisions, let your family know. Some people have a special family meeting and invite the attorney, the accountant, and/or the financial professional. Consider that these people are going to meet with your family someday anyway, but likely under more stressful circumstances. Introducing them as part of the planning process is yet another gift you can give.

Self-Assessment: Estate Planning

Do I have my five basic estate planning documents in place? If not, what has prevented me from completing this task? _____

_____

*If so, are the documents older than five years? (If yes, have them reviewed for changes in tax law, case law, and your personal circumstances.)*_____

Were the documents drafted in the same state in which I now reside? (If not, make sure new ones are drafted according to your current state statutes.) _____

Unplanned Sharing: Lending Versus Giving

"Will you lend me some money?" Sometimes we see it coming, and sometimes we don't. Among the most common types of unplanned sharing is the loan to a friend, family member, subordinate, or employee. Often, the borrower asks for a loan because he or she does not want to ask for an outright gift. Some borrowers have full intentions of repaying. Others do not. Still others think they will repay somehow, but never do.

Ironically, as a friend, employer, or relative, we are not always best suited to know others' intentions and actions as borrowers; it is precisely these kinds of relationships that can cloud our judgment. Unless you have been in the lending business, it can be very difficult to predict any borrower's ability and willingness to repay a loan.

A loan will change a relationship. It will lurk alongside your friendship, your family connection, or your employer-employee relationship. For some borrowers, the obligation is a burden that will drive them to repay the loan as quickly as possible. For others, the obligation weighs on their conscience; but lacking the ability to repay, they accumulate guilt and shame about it. This changes their behavior in the relationship, possibly causing anger, passive-aggressiveness, or avoidance of contact with you. For still others, the loan might as well have been a gift and is no burden on their conscience at all. The behavior change occurs then in the lender rather than the borrower. Regardless, a loan can sow the seeds of resentment, guilt, and embarrassment in both parties.

If you both decide to go ahead with a loan, formalize the arrangement in writing so that expectations are clear on both sides. If the loan is for purchasing real estate, you can look into National Family Mortgage (www.nationalfamilymortgage.com) for guidance. Another option is www.nolo.com, which is a site with no-cost or low-cost legal documents. It is best to hire an attorney to draft a promissory note and lien documents to cover and formalize the details.

Consider responding to a loan request with a gift decision instead. A gift is a one-sided transaction. It comes with no expectations. Assuming you are the giver, ask yourself if you would have given the requester the money anyway? It's okay if the answer is no. No matter which response you make, once the request is made, the relationship is permanently altered. Regardless of whether you say yes or no, the emotional effects of making a gift decision are not revisited with every interaction as they might be with a loan.

If the gift decision is made, the giver should let the recipient know what to expect in the future. Establish whether the gift is a one-time offering or the first of other possible gifts. Reducing the mystery can benefit both the giver and the recipient and reduce the chances of an expectations-resentment cycle from growing.

Giving a gift for something you are passionate about can bring long-lasting satisfaction. Make it your policy not to give loans. Let gifts suffice.

Self-Assessment: Lending Versus Giving

A time when I loaned someone money: _____

_____

_____

How did it work out? What was the result? _____

_____

_____

How did I feel when I made the loan? _____

_____

_____

Was it paid back? _____

_____

_____

How did I feel afterward? _____

_____

_____

Did I feel that my relationship with the recipient changed as a result of the loan? _____

_____

_____

How is that relationship today? _____

_____

_____

Would I loan money again? _____

Can I make a loan without strings attached or judgments about lifestyle choices? _____

When I am asked for a loan, I will now respond with: _____

_____

_____

Mindfully Prepared with a Plan

At this point in the book, especially if you have worked on the self-assessments, you are equipped with a more mindful money mentality.

You have examined your money messages. You have considered your principles for saving, spending, and sharing. You have intentionally identified and quantified needs, comforts, and luxuries of several different kinds. You have considered charitable giving. You have thought about how money might contribute to, rather than detract from, your happiness.

So guess what? You have built the foundation for a well-thought-out, mindful financial lifestyle plan.

The next job will be to put in place a mindful money management system. It may be one that you create and administer yourself, although for most people, the help of a professional will be in order. Either way, to keep your mindful money mentality, it will be valuable to understand the obstacles, both internal and external, that can prevent you from achieving success.

Part II, next, is all about mindful money management and you.

PART II

MINDFUL MONEY MANAGEMENT AND YOU

5

Mindful Financial Planning and Investing

"Everything should be made as simple as possible, but no simpler."
~Composer Roger Sessions, paraphrasing Albert Einstein ("How a Difficult
Composer Gets That Way", The New York Times, January 8, 1950)

Financial Lifestyle Planning

When you think of a "financial plan," what comes to mind? Budgets? Investments? IRAs? Retirement plans? For most people and for some advisors, a financial plan may consist of a pie chart and a list of mutual funds that took no more than an hour to produce.

One problem with keeping our sights too narrowly focused on a financial plan is it can create unnecessary risk, but not the growth-inducing financial kind. Doing this kind of narrow financial planning is like thinking you can stay healthy simply by exercising but not by paying attention to what you eat. In the short run, things may look good, but down the road, something will indeed go wrong.

A basic comprehensive financial plan should include all of the following:

- Cash flow/budgeting/analysis of income sources and expenses
- Investments
- Income taxes
- Retirement planning
- Insurance (life, health, long-term care, disability, and property/casualty) planning
- College and other education planning
- Estate planning

You might also consider these:

- Banking and cash management
- Annuities review: fixed versus variable
- Executive benefits, including stock options and deferred compensation
- Business continuation plans
- Business cash management
- Charitable planning and giving
- Lifetime gifts to family
- Kids and money
- Rental real estate
- Family and third party partnerships

If done mindfully, a financial plan will take much longer than an hour to create. Your planner needs to understand your approach to money, your principles, and your goals for needs, wants, and wishes. (Your completion of the self-assessments from earlier chapters here will save both you and your planner a lot of time.) The mindful financial planner will want to understand the big picture of the life you want to live. Once you have that big picture, you'll have more than a financial plan.

You'll have a financial *lifestyle* plan. A financial lifestyle plan is a fluid document, reviewed periodically and/or in response to life events.

With this understanding, your planner can begin to craft the investment strategy component of your plan. Much of investing, unlike saving, spending, and sharing, is beyond our immediate control, which makes staying mindful about it doubly difficult. Although this can be a difficult concept to grasp at first, much more detail will be provided below.

A financial lifestyle plan really encompasses *all* of your money decisions: saving, spending, sharing, and investing. While Chapter 4 focused on saving, spending, and sharing, Chapter 5 will focus solely on investing.

The Mystery of the Investing World

How many of us enjoy hearing that anything in life, particularly relating to our money, is beyond our control?

When I first began learning about investments in the early 1990s, it seemed mysterious but chic. At the bank where I worked, I listened to the investment gurus talk to clients about stocks and bonds. They sounded terribly smart. But I soon learned that they really had no special powers after all. When they did well, they took credit. When they did not do well, they said it was "beyond their control." Later I learned that it was nearly *always* beyond their control. But clients do not want to hear this, and some professionals do not want to think it, much less say it.

I didn't come to this realization without going through my own painful discovery process first. The first time I dipped my toe into that dark, mysterious world was when I bought a hot stock called Enron. (Remember Enron?) Then I invested in a friend's startup bank, which later failed. I started out in the investing world 0-for-2. It's not hard to see that those early investments are where many people first get bogged down, confused, and frustrated. It's also where they experience their first losses.

Some people have a mailbox and an emailbox full of various statements from different companies. They don't know which companies are "bad," and which ones are "good." The potpourri of accounts and statements share no coherent objective tied to their owner's long-term well-being.

Other people (the newbie investors) continually shop the CD rates, closing one account and opening another. Going from bank to bank, they spend entire days completing forms and shopping for rates, while their mailboxes fill with maturity notices.

Yet others attempt to gain control through knowledge. They keep the financial news networks on all the time. They spend hours online searching for investing answers. They follow gurus. They read investing books. They know their exact net worth as of the closing bell. But they still feel as if they are on their own and even lost.

Sometimes, people listen to the successful investing stories of friends, family, and neighbors, hoping they too can benefit from the next product/fund/brainiac nirvana of investing.

And sometimes, people just plain panic. Doing something feels better than doing nothing. We sell everything at the bottom. We get greedy. We buy it back at the top. We get excited. We buy gold. We get anxious. We sell gold. Stuck in our infinite loop, we circle like a pond waterbug. Doing something after something after something without any direction leads us ever deeper into frustration. And if we turn to certain professionals for help, we can end up being locked into products we do not completely understand. More regret. The statements keep coming in the mailbox. We're in a vicious cycle.

How did this happen? What can we do? Who will care besides us?

Being worry-free about investing is truly more about making a series of rational, informed decisions than about beating the Dow Jones Industrial Average. It comes from understanding how certain types of money can be expected to behave. It is not really about finding the right financial product or investment guru, although our society certainly makes it out to be.

Investment statements show *short-term* results. They do not tell you how those results will affect your long-term odds of financial success. If you looked at your portfolio value every minute of the day, and were happy when it was greater and unhappy when it was less so, how emotionally drained would you be after twelve hours?

Individual investments, and investment advisors, inevitably fail to meet constant positive-return expectations. Chasing this rainbow, both the professionals and the investors make two major errors: focusing backwards on the wrong goal, and spending time and energy on decisions that will not make a difference in the long run.

In fact, it may be far more realistic to expect that certain investments will zig while others will zag, and if you keep the zigs and zags in mindful, consistent, strategic proportion, you will succeed.

A Mindful Investment Plan

Like the USDA's nutrition icon, a plate sectioned into the four food groups, investments can be divided into four asset groups:

1. Cash
2. Stocks
3. Bonds
4. Other

For each of these groups, there are five basic principles to apply and keep in mind when investing:

- First Principle: Get the mix right.
- Second Principle: Let it stew.
- Third Principle: Stocks; own all, not some.
- Fourth Principle: Bonds; own some, not all.
- Fifth Principle: Rebalance regardless regularly.

First Principle: Get the Mix Right

A mix of the four asset groups will determine most of your investing success in the long run. Based upon your stated goals and resources, your financial lifestyle plan should tell you how much of each "food group" you need on your plate. It is not important whether you pick broccoli (for example, IBM stock) or cauliflower (say, Intel stock) for the produce (stocks) portion, but that you get the relative portion on the plate correct.

In other words, the most important investment decision you can make is all about the relative percentage that you allocate to cash, stocks, bonds, and other. This is called your "asset allocation."

The asset allocation recommended for you should not come from a laminated pie chart pulled out of an advisor's desk drawer. It should be the considered result of a process that is meant to maximize the odds of your success.

For example, a mix of 65% stocks/30% bonds/5% cash might give you an 85% chance for success in meeting your shelter, transportation, travel, and toy goals at their ideal levels. But a mix of 60% stocks/35% bonds/5% cash might increase those odds to 90%.

There is a nifty software tool you can use to test for your best allocation: it's called the Monte Carlo simulator. Basic versions are available online. There are also financial planners who have invested in the software and can make the Monte Carlo an integral part of their service to you. Make sure you ask any potential advisors how they are going to derive their recommendations for your asset allocation.

Second Principle: Let It Stew

The first three—cash, stocks, and bonds—of these four groups behave randomly over short periods of time and predictably (within a range) over long periods of time. So a major part of your success will lie in allowing them the time needed to do what they will do. The fourth group—other—should consist of assets that behave randomly over both short and long periods of time. We will look further at why this might or might not be a good thing later on in this chapter.

Third Principle: Own All, Not Some

Your asset allocation will tell you how much of your portfolio should be invested in stocks.

Owning a stock represents owning a very small percentage (or "share") of a company. If the company declares a dividend (a return of profit to the shareholders), a shareholder receives his or her proportionate share of that dividend. If the company appears to have bright prospects for profits, and therefore for paying more dividends in the future, other investors will want to own that stock and the price will go up. As an existing shareholder in that company, you'll enjoy the stock's "appreciation" as the price increases, plus you'll get dividends. Dividends + Appreciation = Return, in the world of stocks. (But take note: Not all stocks will pay dividends, and certainly, not all stocks will appreciate.)

When we look back over long periods of time, we see that stocks have provided higher returns than any other asset group. However, those higher returns have always come with higher risk. Risk in "favorable" markets tells us how much might be gained. In "unfavorable" markets, it gives us an idea of how much might be lost. The basic rule is, to get higher long-term returns, stockholders have to endure higher risk.

The thing to be aware of about risk is, we can say we can handle risk as long as we get a return. But risk is felt more acutely during unfavorable markets than during favorable ones. As we'll see in Chapter 7, the pain we feel from losses often exceeds the pleasure we get from gains. It can be emotionally difficult to stick with our plans through the losses when gains are nowhere in sight.

Stocks never come with promises of dividends or growth. There is no protection from losses and no guarantee of principal. At different times in history, certain kinds of stocks, and sometimes all stocks at once, have been subject to speculative bubbles that finally burst, causing the market to crash.

Yet, we must return to the fact that, in the long run, stocks produce returns that beat inflation. The assets that are the riskiest generally do provide the highest returns.

Your asset allocation will further divide your stock proportion into different kinds of stock categories like "large," "small," and/or "international." Picking individual stocks in each category is what "active" investors and money managers do. Rather than selecting individual company stocks, it can be easier and/or less costly to own all of them within a single category, or as close to all of them as you can get. Owning all stocks in a category, or close to all, is called "passive" investing. Because all of the stocks in a category are represented by an "index," another term for passive investing is "buying the index."

You have two choices about what kind of stock strategy you want to employ: active or passive. You also have two choices about who can do this work: you could do it yourself until you are about 80 (an age at which half of us begin to lose the cognitive wherewithal to manage money) or hire someone else. Of course, you could also do a combination of these, managing some yourself and hiring others to help. This book is geared to keeping your investing decisions simple. You are best served to pick an investment approach you believe will be best for you. If you hire a professional, discuss your preferred strategy and reasoning. Hear the professional out if he or she doesn't agree with you, and, using the techniques discussed in the following chapters, decide if you want to change course. The most important thing is to find what you believe in and stick to it.

This now means there are four combinations of approaches (if you're younger than 80): Active Do-It-Yourself; Passive Do-It-Yourself; Active Hire Someone; or Passive Hire Someone. So how do you choose?

Suppose there is a year like 2010 when stocks rose 17%. Pretend it is December 2010 and your asset allocation, which, for example, is supposed to have 65% stocks, has risen to 76% stocks. What do you do?

Ignoring any tax effects for the moment, theoretically, since your portfolio is now out of balance, you should rebalance: sell some of your assets (stocks) that have risen in value, and buy the ones (bonds) that have gone down.

But this can be harder to do than it sounds. It may in fact seem counterintuitive to sell something that is doing well. (Again, as we will see in Chapter 7, it's actually counter *emotional*, too!) And to buy something that has gone down? Even more so.

And how do you know which stocks to pick? This is where the active/passive question enters the picture, since answering this question is the source of great debate in the financial industry.

My advice is not to try Active Do-It-Yourself. It can be disheartening, if you've spent years studying Warren Buffett, reading company annual reports, and watching analyst recommendations, to realize that your efforts have resulted in no appreciable benefit. Indeed, it is disheartening to a good many financial professionals, too, who make their living believing and preaching otherwise.

Active Hire Someone could mean to hire an investment manager who will pick stocks and/or mutual funds for you, or it could mean to buy an actively-managed mutual fund (since you would be hiring the fund manager). Bear in mind, however, that far fewer than 50% of active mutual fund managers meet the basic expectation of their job: to pick better stocks than an investor could do by buying the relevant passive index. One study by Vanguard Investments showed that between 5% and 55% of active fund managers outperformed their assigned benchmark index over a 15-year period.[1]

If you decided you wanted to buy an actively-managed fund, how would you find the 5% to 55% of managers who succeeded? If we were to look at a three-year or ten-year period, there might be different managers who were "successful" for different periods of time. Much research shows it is difficult to pick the best active managers in advance. Nevertheless, there are professionals who appear to be skilled at doing so.

For purposes of this book, buying the index that a majority of managers are trying so hard, and failing, to beat, is the simplest solution. One simple, if dull, strategy is to invest in the widest possible diversified portfolio. The ultimate recommendation from your plan will provide more detail on the proportion of large companies, small companies, U.S. companies, or foreign companies. To acquire each of these, you can purchase either an "index fund," or an "exchange-traded fund" that covers every stock in each of these categories; both types of funds do this for very low cost. This would fall into either Passive Do-It-Yourself (if you selected the actual funds yourself) or Passive Hire Someone (if you hired someone to select the funds for you).

The next chapter will include questions to ask yourself before deciding whether to do it yourself or hire a professional for all, or part, of your money management.

Fourth Principle: Own Some, Not All

For bonds, it isn't possible to own all of them in a single category because the supply of bonds is more limited than stocks. Although you can passively invest in bonds through index funds, the funds are not actually a collection of all of the bonds in the index. Bond indexes are only an approximation of the bond market. (Stock indexes, by contrast, hold all of the actual securities in that segment of the stock market.) It is best to own a large number of individual bonds. But this is not always prudent if you do not have a lot of money to diversify them sufficiently, or if your money is tied up in an employer's retirement plan like a 401(k) or 403(b).

In the simplest terms, bonds reduce risk. Unlike stocks and mutual funds, bonds have maturity dates. As long as the bond issuer does not default, the bond buyer can expect the principal back on the maturity date. And until the maturity date, unless it is a "zero coupon" bond, the bond buyer will also get periodic interest payments.

But be aware that just because bonds will return a stated value on the maturity date, they won't necessarily keep that same value from their issuance until their maturity. The time between a bond's issuance and its maturity can be anywhere from two to 30 years. During that time, many factors can reduce or increase the market's perceived value of the bond. Just as with stocks, it will be difficult to be content to hold on to them while this happens. The factor with the greatest impact on value is the bond's stated interest rate, or "coupon."

Here is a hypothetical example to illustrate:

In year 1, assume your investment manager buys a $10,000 bond paying a 5% coupon that matures in five years. That means you are earning 5% x $10,000, or $500 in interest per year.

In year 2, interest rates rise to 7% (not a common occurrence in a 12-month period of time, but good enough to make the point). Your bond is no longer very attractive to the market because it is paying only 5%. You open your investment statement showing your bond (originally purchased for $10,000) is now worth just $7,140. You are not happy. However, your financial planner told you this might happen, so you keep collecting your $500 interest payments on your $10,000 bond.

Two years later, in year 4, interest rates fall to 4%. Your 5% bond now looks terrific. You open your statement and learn that your bond is now worth $12,500. You first thought you wanted to sell it back in year 2, but now, you really want to sell it. Problem is, when you collect your $12,500, you can only reinvest it at 4%. You already have something paying 5%. Your financial planner tells you once again to stay the course.

Year 5 arrives, and you get your $10,000, plus you've been getting 5% interest for the past five years. You might say to your planner, "This is nothing to write home about. It's boring. This is not growth."

The planner might reply, "Exactly. It's safety: plain, simple, and predictable."

No matter what value fluctuations the bond experiences between issuance and maturity, it will still pay $10,000 on the maturity date, as long as the issuer does not default. In good times, you may feel foolish for making such a boring investment. In bad times, you may feel immense relief that you made such a safe investment. (Welcome to the bond market!)

It's also important to understand that bonds come with different and important features and characteristics. To list and explain them all takes entire textbooks. Also note that there is no FDIC insurance on bonds; you can lose principal on them. (If they did not have more risk than bank accounts, they would yield the same rates as bank accounts. Such is the law of risk and return: there is no free lunch.) Even after extensive study of these funds, the use of information in the real bond market takes practice and experience.

This now brings us to the question of how you would make bonds a part of your portfolio. One option for doing it yourself is to open an account with Treasury Direct. This is a tool allowing you to buy U.S. Treasury bonds directly from the United States Treasury. The site where you can do this, www.treasurydirect.gov, is relatively straightforward, and the menu of available bonds is easy to navigate. You could build a "ladder" of Treasury bonds for which you pick successive maturity dates, collect the principal, and then reinvest each time a bond matures. One disadvantage of an all-Treasury bond portfolio is that Treasuries, while they are considered the safest bonds on the market (in terms of low likelihood of default), also pay the lowest coupons. They are a low-risk, low-return investment, then.

Also, even though the U.S. government is considered the "safest" (and dullest?) issuer of all, there is something to be said about having all bonds with just one safe issuer.

When it comes to non-Treasury bonds, their features—like credit ratings, call-options, tax-exempt issues, zero coupons, and so on—make buying them wisely a matter of much practice, and mistakes can be very costly. Ideally, you would buy bonds at a "discount" (always an attractive word in purchasing), which in finance means you buy them for less than the stated value. (In the illustrative example above, for example, you might buy the bond for $7,140 when it is out of favor and then collect $10,000, or "par" value, at maturity, although such wide disparities in value and par are not frequent or expected.) Ideally, you would also know how to read the issuers' financial statements and come to your own judgment about the credit rating. Buying bonds takes skill and experience. If you are not going to buy all Treasuries, you should ideally find a bond manager with the desire, experience, and expertise in bonds to assist you. (See the Sidebar: Bond Managers for information on hiring a bond manager.)

Bond Managers

How do you pick a bond manager? There are four ways: 1. Buy a bond manager's mutual fund; 2. Buy a bond index fund; 3. Hire a "retail" bond manager; or 4. Hire a "wholesale" bond manager.

Buying a bond mutual fund or bond index fund sounds like the easiest way to go. But they both have one major drawback: neither has a maturity date.

Bond managers are individuals, or companies, who will buy a portfolio of individual bonds for you. Retail bond managers can be found at any retail brokerage. Unfortunately there is no designation for "certified" bond managers, but a good designation/prerequisite would be a Chartered Financial Analyst (CFA). The CFA credential means analysts have the education to make their own judgments about credit ratings.

If there is a particular CFA you're interested in, you would ask about his or her experience with managing bonds, philosophy about purchasing at premiums versus discounts, about holding until maturity, and about cost structure. Ideally the manager would be compensated only by the fees you pay him or her, not by hidden commissions or "markups" on trading bonds. The ideal manager would also have access to bonds at a wholesale or "institutional" desk. If you are dealing with a trust company, for example, you will most likely be assigned a bond manager who purchases bonds wholesale.

The ideal answers to your questions to a bond manager would sound something like these:

1. I have more than ten years of experience managing individual bonds, and I have a CFA designation.

2. My philosophy is to purchase bonds at discounts as frequently as possible.

3. My practice is to hold bonds until maturity. I generally do not sell bonds before maturity unless I judge there is too great a default risk.

4. Either I charge a fee of no more than 1.0% for managing bonds; or my markups amount to less than 1.0%. I do not charge both a fee and a markup on bonds. Any markups will be fully disclosed to you.

The reason I distinguish between the two types "retail" and "wholesale" is that the supply of bonds is a lot like the supply of prime steak. Much of the time, prime grades of steak never make it to the retail grocery store because the steakhouse restaurants will have bought the entire supply. Retail customers at the grocery still get choice grade, but only occasionally is prime available.

Similarly, the prime bonds are often purchased first by institutions, leaving the choice bonds for the retail brokers and their clients. If you are dealing with a wholesale bond manager, that manager will have access to a better inventory of bonds for you. This is not to say retail brokers cannot find appropriate bonds that will achieve your objectives, only that they may have a more difficult time of it, particularly in a tight bond market where the supply and demand of bonds are very close.

If your bond manager works for a brokerage firm that also underwrites and/or holds bonds, you have a two-edged sword. On one hand, the manager should get you the first pick of bond issues underwritten by his or her firm, to which other bond managers may not have access. On the other hand, the firm could induce or pressure the manager to sell you its own bonds, which may be suitable but may not be the best for you.

In other words, if your bond manager works for a firm that underwrites bonds, he or she has a conflict of interest. This conflict, and how the manager handles it, should be disclosed to you, both verbally and in writing.

In your research on buying bonds, you may come across a manager who has a fancy whiz-bang bond strategy. There are many complex bond-buying strategies, not for the security of receiving back the principal on the maturity date, but for speculation on their values between issuance and maturity. Such strategies may be appropriate for large college endowments and wealthy individuals who know how much they can afford to speculate. But for the purposes of this presentation, such strategies run counter to the basic objective of minimizing your odds of running out of money.

So if bonds are so great, then why not invest everything in a diversified portfolio of bonds and forget about stocks? It's because bonds come with a loss guarantee: as long as we have inflation, bonds held for principal protection are guaranteed to lose purchasing power. Just like an all-protein diet does not provide nutritional balance, an all-bonds diet will not protect you from inflation.

Alternatives or "Other Food Groups"

Anyone who cooks knows that butter, salt, and pepper make almost anything taste good. But what if you add every spice on the shelf to the stew?

In the "other" category of investing, there are assets like gold, real estate, commodities, futures, oil and gas, private equity, hedge funds, and venture capital. Because of their unique characteristics as categories unto themselves, they are known in industry lingo as "alternative investments." Like spices used artfully, they can turn an average portfolio into a sensational one. Used in overabundance or in the wrong combination, they'll also be sensational, but not in the ways we want.

Getting the timing and proportion of alternative investments right is a job only a handful of professionals have mastered. As with successful active stock managers, these professionals can be difficult to find.

Nevertheless, because we all encounter the seemingly brilliant alternative asset stories often enough, it's important to share a few words about them.

These investments don't behave like stocks and bonds. They tend to have greater volatility (higher highs and lower lows), and/or longer cycles to grow and recover. Many of them require tying up your principal with no way to return it for several years. To many financial professionals, these are good things: they call this behavior "uncorrelated." Mostly this means that when everything else is in a nosedive, your alternative investments will be holding steady or gaining.

The year 2008 was the big test for alternative investments. Some performed exactly as they were designed to. Many did not. Finding the ones that did perform well, and assuming they would continue to, was in itself a job for the professionals.

On top of being difficult to predict, alternatives can be expensive and inconvenient to purchase, maintain, and/or sell. Take, for example, real estate, commodities, (physical) gold, collectibles, hedge, and private equity funds. The first four do not pay interest or dividends; and gold and collectibles must be stored and protected, adding extra costs for ownership. Instead of the management fees of less than 1% that you can expect on the stock and bond options discussed above, one typical compensation scheme for hedge and private equity funds is "2 and 20." This means the manager collects 2% of your account per year, plus 20% of the profits the fund makes.

One way to keep costs down and convenience up is to purchase exchange-traded funds or index funds that specialize in one of the above single categories. Many managers argue that today's portfolios are not complete without one or more of these categories.

Back again in the food world, spice adds no nutritional value. But in the investing world, a nutritious portfolio, from which you can get a "balanced meal," is one that sticks to cash, stocks, and bonds. Like spice, alternatives can be nice, but not always necessary.

Fifth Principle: Rebalance Regardless Regularly

After you have your initial allotted portions of cash, stocks, bonds, and "other" in place, the proportions will change. Like the landscaping in the yard, the portfolio will need some trimming and pruning. A mindfully simple investing strategy is to look at your allocations every three months, every six months, or every year, and see what may have grown to more than its allotted portion. You can sell the part that is excessive and buy in an area where you are short. This is called "rebalancing."

Rational investors rebalance, regardless, regularly. (Say that ten times very fast!) The difficult but beautiful key to investing is like the old Serenity Prayer: accept what you cannot change, change what you can, and, with wisdom, know the difference. You cannot change, control, or manipulate the investment markets any more than you can control the menu at a restaurant (unless you own it!). You can control the choices you make. You can control your goals and how happy you will be with the trade-offs you make. You can control how often you prune and trim your portfolio by scheduling these on your calendar. Rebalancing according to a regular schedule, regardless of what is happening in the markets or in the news, will give you the discipline and confidence you need to be successful.

Notes:

1. Page 90: Philips, Christopher B., CFA, Francis M. Kinniry, Jr., CFA, and Todd Schlanger, "The case for index investing," The Vanguard Group, April 2013, Figure 2, p. 6.

6

Delegating Money Management

"We are what we repeatedly do. Excellence, then, is not an act, but a habit." ~Aristotle

Two Different Clients

Diana came to the meeting armored and ready for financial battle, her boyfriend by her side for moral support. Whatever damage I was planning to inflict on her, she was prepared for and ready to fight.

Sam arrived and spilled his brokerage statements onto the table even before I could say, "Good morning." Shoulders hunched, head down, he was discouraged, done in, defeated, and sure that he would never figure out the world of investments. I could have given him random lottery numbers as advice and he might have taken them.

What was it that made Diana and Sam so different? How did one arrive so sure that a war would ensue with a financial professional, while the other, so trusting, came so ready to capitulate?

Where might you fall along the spectrum between Diana and Sam? What is your approach to financial professionals: defensive? suspicious?

over trusting? cautiously optimistic? To remain mindful as you begin interviewing and then hiring a financial professional, try to understand that how we approach the search—whether we project positive or negative energy—can determine not only our own attitudes but the responses we receive.

Personal Experience with Professionals

What exactly can a professional add to your money management quest that you don't already have yourself? First, think of these professionals as if they were architects. At several points in our lives, my husband and I interviewed architects about building us a custom-designed house. The ones we felt most comfortable with not only asked the usual questions about how many bedrooms and bathrooms we wanted and how big our budget was; they wanted to know who we were. We saw that if we didn't know ourselves and were unclear about what we wanted, then the architect could not do his job. His questions forced us to do some serious mental homework in order to get to exactly what kind of living quarters we wanted.

Later, after we had built our house, we remembered the trade-offs we had made and the reasons behind them. I sometimes wondered if we had asked the architect to make all our decisions for us whether we would have been resentful and frustrated with his choices, not ours. If I had not been so involved in the design, I certainly would not have understood the mutual exclusivity of certain structural, material, and finish decisions. I would not have been familiar with our own emotions around small things, too, like window treatments.

How about you? How do you approach a professional relationship and your expectations for it? For starters, try this self-assessment:

Self-Assessment

Think about both good and bad experiences I have had with these professionals: attorneys, accountants, bankers, insurance agents, investment managers, stockbrokers, and/or trust officers.

Describe the good experiences: _____
_____
_____
_____

Describe the bad experiences: _____
_____
_____
_____

Are there any common themes? Can the "goodness" or "badness" of each experience be laid at the feet of the professional, or did I play a part in the quality of the final outcome? _____
_____
_____
_____

Before hiring a professional, I should ask myself these questions:

On Roles and Strategy

If my money were a ship carrying me to my destination, would I be more comfortable as the owner of the ship, as its captain, or as its first mate? OR, simply as its passenger? _____

How much do I enjoy making my own investing decisions? _____
_____

Will my investments be managed according to a strict system, or handled with flexibility? _____

_____

On Discipline

What is my track record on sticking to a plan? _____

_____

If I am creating and implementing a plan by myself, how will I measure my results? _____

_____

How often and how closely do I read the prospectuses that come with mutual funds and other investment products? _____

_____

On Teamwork

How well will I coordinate my investments with my accountant's tax advice? _____

_____

Has a lack of coordination among business, tax, insurance, and legal issues ever hurt me before? _____

_____

How well do I understand the impact of my estate plan on my investments, and vice versa? _____

_____

On Peace of Mind

How much do thoughts about money decisions enter into my leisure time?

_____

Considering all of the above, would I hire me? _____

_____

If your answer to that last question is a definite yes, then you may be in the modest ten percent of individuals who are able to manage their finances, including investments, without any outside help.

If you have turned to a professional in the past and been disappointed, it may be the professional's fault, but you yourself may also have played a role in the disappointing outcome. If you were not able to communicate where you were going or what you wanted and needed, did you really expect the professional to define these for you and help you get there? Advisors, like physicians, do the best they can with the information we give them.

Finding the right professional fit is crucial for most people. Professional help can replace fear, worry, and regret with peace of mind. That said— and I speak from more than 25 years in the financial industry—there are far too many people who were misguided by financial professionals.

A 5-Point Test for Finding Financial Professionals

By the time you go shopping for your financial professional, you will have done a lot of the preparatory work in this book. You will know your money history: its messages and flashpoints, your beliefs and habits. You will have thought about both your ideal and acceptable attainment of goals, the resources you have for your plan, and all of the costs and incentives you are up against. Whoever you choose should be delighted with your well-thought-out preparations, your goals, dreams, and desires.

The quality of information and advice available in the financial advisory business varies greatly, just as it does in architecture, medicine, and business management. Most important are the quality and scope of the information and advice, dispensed objectively and with your best interests in mind. Here is a 5-point test of attributes to look for in a financial professional.

1. He or she possesses the right background and credentials for your needs.

2. He or she embraces a fiduciary duty to you.

3. He or she will work transparently, fully disclosing all costs, conflicts, and compensation.

4. He or she has done a personal financial plan and knows his or her own money messages.

5. He or she will address your plan comprehensively.

In this chapter, we will examine what each of these means, how you can recognize them all, and how you can use them to find the best professional for you.

TEST 1: Possesses the Right Background and Credentials

The Credentials Alphabet

Here is a bit of wisdom from the Financial Industry Regulatory Authority (FINRA):

> "Be aware that Financial Analyst, Financial Advisor (Adviser), Financial Consultant, Financial Planner, Investment Consultant, or Wealth Manager are generic terms or job titles, and may be used by investment professionals who may not hold any specific designation." (from the FINRA Investor Information website, www.finra.org)

You probably understand the differences between a general medical practitioner, a heart surgeon, a nutritionist, a neurologist, and a pharmacist. The medical industry, fortunately, provides us with titles, certifications, and designations that help us understand who does what. Unfortunately, the financial industry has not yet evolved to the point of standardized nomenclature and certifications that can be widely understood.

So how do you tell the differences between financial professionals, their designations, and the letters and titles on their business cards?

The Wall Street Journal reported in November 2010 that it found more than 200 credentials in the financial industry.[1] No wonder there is so much confusion about them! FINRA's dropdown list at https://apps. finra.org/DataDirectory/1/prodesignations.aspx provides information on 117 industry certifications so that investors can see who issues them, whether they have met specific standards for accreditation, and what continuing education and exams are required to maintain them.

Interestingly, *The Wall Street Journal* also found three credentialing organizations on the FINRA list that were led by individuals who had disciplinary actions filed against them. If the organization granting the credential doesn't have standards for its leadership, then what credit can you give the credential?

The most rigorous of the 117 designations listed by FINRA are:

- LL.M. (Master of Laws)
- CFA (Chartered Financial Analyst)
- CPA (Certified Public Accountant),
- and CFP® (Certified Financial Planner; this is a registered title, which we'll examine below).

The LL.M. is a designation acquired by lawyers after they complete an additional year of law school. The CFA exams test a year's worth of knowledge every year for three years. Only about half of those who take the CPA and CFP® exams, which take place over two days, pass on the first try. The knowledge they require covers a broad range of subjects, and both the CPA and the CFP® certifications as of 2010 also require a four-year college degree as a prerequisite. There are many determined people who have made five, seven, or even ten attempts to achieve a CFA, CPA, or a CFP®.

Passing the exams is only the beginning for those who want to claim these designations. All require many continuing education hours (30 annually for CFP®s, and typically around 40 annually for CPAs depending on their state of licensure). And the certifying boards are strict about what constitutes acceptable continuing education courses.

By contrast, one of the easier designations to obtain is the Accredited Asset Management Specialist, or AAMS, the certification I received before attaining my CFP®. It has no prerequisites. It required about 20 hours of self-study and then a single exam that I completed in about an hour. The material was not difficult. I did learn quite a bit from the process, but once I received the credential, it required no further education of me at all.

Among the other 112 designations on FINRA's site, some only require that a potential candidate send them a check to be registered. Would you feel comfortable entrusting your life's savings to someone whose professional credential required only a cleared bank check? Likely not. Yet, when professionals put letters of any kind on their business cards, they do so knowing that most consumers have little idea what the letters mean or whether they even represent the four listed above. (Have you ever encountered "Pat Smith, CXC, CZZR®, MBA, ABCD-QR" and wondered what in the world ...?) Considering our tendency to take shortcuts (more on this in Chapter 7), is it any wonder why some consumers consider the quantity of letters as an indication of quality?

The public is as much to blame for not demanding better information and clearer signs of credentialing as the industry is for taking advantage of it.

Defining Your Professional's Role

The Certified Financial Planner Board of Standards has trademarked the use of the CFP® designation. This means that no professional can legally present him—or herself as a Certified Financial Planner® unless he or she has met the board's requirements, including passage of the exam. Still, this doesn't prevent many uncredentialed advisors from dropping the "Certified" from the title, thus increasing public confusion.

Like medical professionals, financial professionals can be generalists or specialists. Since there is no accepted standard terminology for titles, we could define the title "financial planner" (preferably one with a CFP® designation) as a focused generalist whose work is to guide, develop and implement your financial lifestyle plan according to a process similar to the one we reviewed at the end of Chapter 1. "Investment manager" could be a specialist in picking investments according to a predetermined asset allocation. "Financial administrator" might be a specialist in keeping your financial life organized. And any of these might be termed a "financial advisor," the most general term of all, referring to anyone who provides any type of financial advice.

Personal CFOs

When your needs in your financial life are deeper or broader than what we have covered so far, you might want to explore a special kind of financial planner, like a personal CFO. Ideally, your supporting cast of professionals—accountant, investment manager, attorney, banker, insurance agent, realtor, financial administrator, and so on— understand how their specialized advice fits within your plan and they will tailor their advice accordingly. Realistically, it may not be feasible or desirable for any of them to serve as the central coordinator of and repository for your total financial picture. So you may indeed benefit from someone who does not specialize in investments or law or tax preparation, but who has general knowledge of many different areas of finance. That's a personal CFO.

A personal CFO specializes in taking a financial project through the necessary steps from goal definition and discovery, through charitable plan design, asset allocation, investment education, location of the right investment manager, risk assessment, and performance reporting, while monitoring the investment, lawyer, accountant, and insurance professionals to make sure their actions and advice are coordinated. Personal CFOs work with you to assure that your plan is implemented efficiently and economically. They use their experience and contacts to ensure that the financial bases are covered and covered in the right order. He or she is a planning and implementation shepherd, mentor, tutor, and coach.

Personal CFOs could be affiliated with a trust company or a small, fee-only boutique. Your personal CFO must be able to align your interests with his or her own, and strike the delicate balance between your needs and the demands of his or her employer, if any. Because of the scope of the engagement, the boutique providers will often require a retainer, while the trust companies may require a minimum management account size for access to their services. As the central coordinator of your financial life, they are an extra layer of management. Not everyone needs a personal CFO.

Jeff Daniher, a Cincinnati CFP® certificant of Ritter Daniher Financial Advisory, LLC, wrote the following on a national association online discussion board. His comment mirrors the types of tasks a personal CFO would accomplish and the attitude with which he or she would accomplish them:

"Here is a random sampling of what I have done in the last month: 1) created a family budget for a husband and wife who were fighting over spending for three years; 2) analyzed in detail whether a client could afford a third home; 3) helped negotiate a severance package and a new employment agreement for an executive changing jobs; 4) helped a very wealthy divorcing couple amicably iron out the financial aspects of the separation, thus avoiding huge legal bills and any big fights; and 5) explored whether a private foundation or a donor-advised fund made better sense for my client.

We as service providers don't know for sure what we will be doing for clients. But as a client's financial planner, we agree to do 'something' that addresses their financial issues that arise at different points in time, whatever those issues become as their circumstances change. [2]

What can you find out from an ADV?

If you choose to interview a professional at a Registered Investment Advisor (RIA) firm or most brokerage firms, then he or she should provide a copy of Form ADV (the Securities and Exchange Commission's abbreviation for "Advisor") along with "Part 2" in order to be complete. Or, at the SEC's Investment Advisor Registration site (http://www.sec.gov/IAPD), you will find the ADV.

The ADV is one of the richest documents you can find for information on a firm and its individual advisors. Lawyers usually write them, but once you read a few, you will learn a lot by looking at the differences among them. You can discover:

- Whether the advisor went to college (CFP® certificate-holders were not required to have a bachelor's degree before 2010)

- Whether there are compensation methods the advisor did not discuss with you

- Whether there have been any disciplinary actions against the advisor that you may not have found or that were not disclosed elsewhere

- Whether the advisor has a criminal history

- How often the advisor has changed firms or employment in the industry

Do not be timid about asking the advisor any question that comes to mind from your reading of the ADV.

Private banking departments and trust companies and their employees are not regulated by the SEC and are exempt from filing Form ADV. You can still ask any of the questions above or ask for resumes.

TEST 2: Embraces A Fiduciary Duty

A 2009 study by the Rand Corporation found that nearly two-thirds of consumer-investors are under the impression that their financial professionals are fiduciaries, that is, professionals who put their clients' interests ahead of their own when giving advice. Sadly, the vast majority of them are mistaken.

What's a fiduciary and why does it matter?

Fiduciary: "one often in a position of authority who obligates himself or herself to act on behalf of another (as in managing money or property) and assumes a duty to act in good faith and with care, candor, and loyalty in fulfilling the obligation." (*Merriam-Webster's Dictionary of Law* ©1996. Merriam-Webster, Inc.)

This standard of care is similar to that of an attorney or a doctor. Acting in this capacity requires the professional to exercise confidentiality, trust, loyalty to the client/patient, disclosure of conflicts of interest, and full accounting of transactions. The imbalance in the level of knowledge between the professional provider and the client/patient is what creates the need for a fiduciary duty in a profession.

According to The Committee for the Fiduciary Standard (www.thefiduciarystandard.org), there are five core principles of an authentic fiduciary duty in financial advice:

1. Put the client's best interests first.
2. Act with prudence; that is, act with the skill, care, diligence, and good judgment of a professional.
3. Do not mislead clients; provide conspicuous, full, and fair disclosure of all important facts.
4. Avoid conflicts of interest.
5. Fully disclose and fairly manage, in the client's favor, any unavoidable conflicts.

Firms that are regulated by the 1940 Investment Advisers Act are required to exercise a fiduciary duty to clients. As of 2011, there were about 275,000 state-registered professionals working for roughly 12,000 Registered Investment Advisor (RIA) firms, regulated by this act.[3]

Brokerage firms and insurance companies are not regulated by the Investment Advisers Act, and therefore are not required to exercise the same level of duty. In 2011, there were more than 630,000 individuals registered as representatives of broker-dealers, and 411,500 insurance representatives, all held to a less rigorous suitability standard.[4,5]

Suitable: (adj.) "appropriate; proper; fit." (*Collins English Dictionary - Complete & Unabridged 10th Edition*. HarperCollins Publishers. 02 Aug. 2013. <Dictionary.com http://dictionary.reference.com/browse/suitable>)

The investing public is assuming that most professionals are operating as fiduciaries, but the overwhelming majority are not. As noted in a 2009 report issued by a CFA (Chartered Financial Analyst) Institute panel:

> "As a result, investors are forced to choose among financial intermediaries who offer services that appear the same to unsophisticated eyes, but who are subject to very different standards of conduct and legal obligations to the client. Most significantly, investment advisors are required to act in their clients' best interest and disclose all material information, including information about conflicts of interest, whereas brokers are subject to the less rigorous suitability standard and do not have to provide the same extensive disclosures." [6]

Acting like a Fiduciary Versus Being One

There are indeed financial advisors who are held to a suitability standard, but give advice like fiduciaries. That is, they treat their clients as Number One. Many more advisors think they are acting like fiduciaries and may even say they are (when their compliance department isn't listening); but when you look closely, you'll see they aren't.

Here are the first two questions to ask of your candidate professional to see if he or she embraces a fiduciary duty:

1. Are you legally obligated to act in my best interests at all times?

2. What are all of the potential conflicts of interest you may have in working with me?

Compensation Models: Motivations Behind Advisors' Advice

Commission

Pure commission is the traditional business model for insurance agents and stockbrokers. The more transactions, the more money the agent or broker makes. When considering the motivation behind financial advice, this is the classic conflict of interest. Commission-based professionals are not held to a fiduciary duty.

However, just because a broker is compensated on commission does not mean he or she lacks ethics, or will not do what is in your best interests. A good, ethical commission-based broker only suggests trades of products that will fit his or her client's situation in a cost- and tax-beneficial manner.

Many do-it-yourselfers benefit from this kind of service. I had this kind of broker myself for a while. His treatment of my big-picture needs and goals was cursory, but I already had these in place and knew what asset allocation I needed. All I really sought was a professional to make solid suggestions for how to implement my plan. This broker did an admirable job recommending low-cost funds that met my needs. He cut his commissions to the lowest possible level because my account was so low maintenance. He was straightforward in the areas where he felt experienced and candid when he felt out of his depth.

Still, the behavior in this compensation model sometimes resembles that of a scent hunter—an agent or stockbroker always on the "scent" of transactions. The broker working for a broker/dealer or an insurance agency is compensated by selling that organization's products. And somehow (interestingly!) a client's "objectives" always seem to dovetail perfectly with an in-house product!

Because it rewards quantity of transactions over quality, a commission-based model usually leaves little time for the client interviews that can help define unique life goals, nor can it allow for the hours needed to complete a comprehensive, long-term financial lifestyle plan.

The Independent Investor: A Client Story

Kathy and Kyle walked into a brokerage office with questions about a seven-figure inheritance from her father. Not knowing where to turn, they chose the national firm that already held her father's account. The broker at their local branch asked some questions, then produced a pie chart suggesting how to allocate the cash. Kathy and Kyle asked a few questions of the broker, and he answered them. They were going to consider his proposal. As they stood to leave, Kyle thanked the broker and reached for the pie chart. The broker, panicked, grabbed it back, and said, "Oh, no, you can't take that. I need it for my next client." Kathy and Kyle never went back.

Commission-based brokers work best with investors who have already gone through the financial lifestyle planning process; who want to implement the plan with an investment professional; and who want to hear from that professional on a frequent basis with ideas for trades that they can accept or reject. Clients who work best with this advisor type have a level of financial knowledge, understanding, and confidence almost on par with that of the investment professional.

If you lean toward doing investing yourself, by the time you have worked through this book's lifestyle plan exercises and have come up with your own asset allocation strategy, you may feel comfortable that this kind of advice will serve you best, even without the fiduciary standard.

Commission-and-Fee

For most of the 20th century, commission-based compensation was how stockbrokers (known as "registered representatives" in financial industry lingo) earned a living. Today, the percentage of registered representatives working exclusively this way is declining. Brokerage firms large and small are increasingly switching to a commission-and-fee (often confused with fee-only) model. Commission-and-fee is also the business model used by the fastest-growing type of advisor, the independent Registered Investment Advisor (RIA). It provides a consistent, steady stream of income for the advisor and puts the advisor more often—though not always completely—on the same side of the table as the client. Although both registered representatives and RIAs can offer commission-and-fee management, RIAs are the only ones held to a fiduciary standard.

In the commission-and-fee model, the firm charges a flat percentage of the assets being managed. Such fees can range from .5% to 2.0% but typically average 1.0%. The lower end of the range is usually charged for larger accounts or for accounts holding primarily individual bonds. Fees are usually assessed and automatically deducted quarterly. Some commission-and-fee models include the trading costs ("execution costs") of buying and selling investments, while with others the client's account reimburses the firm for these costs.

If the advisor works for a brokerage firm or insurance agency (whether as an employee or as an independent contractor), he or she personally receives a percentage of the fees, which can range from 20% to 90% depending on the employment arrangement with the firm. If the commission-and-fee advisor is on his or her own as an RIA, all of the revenue will go to his or her firm.

In addition, the commission-and-fee advisor, RIA or otherwise, may receive commissions on sales of mutual funds, annuities, or life insurance. These kinds of product-based compensation distinguish a commission-and-fee advisor from a fee-only advisor.

The transition from commission-only to commission-and-fee compensation most often changes control over the account from the client to the advisor. Under most commission-and-fee models, the advisor is given discretion to buy and sell.

When a broker is charging a fee to select and recommend securities and/or mutual funds, the account is commonly called a "wrap" account, because the fee "wraps" around the funds being managed.

What can be difficult to ascertain is the appropriateness of a commission-and-fee advisor's recommendations. The advisor may have an incentive to recommend a fund with a 3% *load* (an upfront sales charge) and .25% *trailer* (a commission received as long as the fund is held by the client) over a fund for which he or she earns no compensation, when both might meet the same objective. Whether or not to charge a load, and how much, is left to the advisor's discretion. However, if the advisor is a Registered Investment Advisor, he or she has a fiduciary duty to recommend what is in the client's best interests, and not something that is merely suitable.

Separately Managed Accounts (SMAs)

If you have more than $500,000 in an investment account, you may be approached about separately managed accounts (SMAs). Separately managed accounts can be cost-superior to mutual funds that have loads or trailers. Some can also be more tax beneficial than mutual funds.

The same statistics about active management from Chapter 5 apply, however: Very few managers truly earn their "keep." Those who do will rapidly accumulate followers and assets under management. They are then left with a dilemma that may have three possible solutions: stop taking new clients; dilute performance by accepting more assets than there are opportunities for investment; or continue accepting assets in the hope that they will continue to be lucrative. So one trick for finding an account manager is to look for managers who will earn their keep before anyone else discovers them! There are financial firms and professionals who focus on finding these managers. But be sure their judgment is not clouded by kickbacks, soft dollars, or other incentives. Examples of such incentives, and how to uncover them, are provided in the rest of this chapter and in Chapter 7.

Withdrawal of Funds

Under the commission-and-fee arrangement, whether using mutual funds or separate accounts, the selecting advisor has an incentive to dissuade you from making large withdrawals—for example, to help a child with a house down payment, or to take a trip, buy a second home or RV, or pay off a mortgage. Such withdrawals reduce the advisor's fees as the money under management shrinks. If your advisor is bound to a fiduciary duty, then he or she must give you the guidance and advice that are in your best interests.

Firms and advisors call the commission-and-fee arrangement "being on the same side of the table" because as the client's assets grow or shrink, so does the firm's compensation, in contrast to other models where the advisor gets paid the same fees regardless of the asset balance.

Many advisors who use the commission-and-fee model are reluctant to switch to the fee-only model because they can easily calculate what they would lose in compensation. This may mean that they will be more expensive than advisors using the fee-only model, but it does not mean they are not worth it. There are commission-and-fee professionals who act like fiduciaries at all times, providing red-carpet customer service; they can be trusted unconditionally with the full knowledge of your and your family's money messages; they will take the time to learn about your lifestyle planning goals; they will stay laser-focused on the odds of meeting those goals as a measure of success; and they will be effective at coaching you through fear, greed, anxiety, and excitement.

Fee-Only

In the fee-only model (often confused with fee-based, another name for commission-and-fee), the advisor receives compensation only from the client, and not from wirehouses, brokerage firms, insurance companies, mutual funds, or any other source. Nearly all fee-only advisors have agreed to be held to a fiduciary standard.

Fee-only advisors can charge in several different ways:

- Through a flat project fee
- Flat annual fee (sometimes called "retainer")

- Hourly
- Through AUM (Assets Under Management) but without trailers and loads

Advisors charging flat fees do so based upon an estimate of how much time and effort they will need to expend to serve a particular client. Flat fees provide predictability of cost for both the advisor and the client. But it is rare today to find advisors who use this method; many find it difficult to predict just how much effort each client will require in a given year.

A number of fee-only advisors bill by the hour. Hourly billing requires more record-keeping, and it may keep you from calling your advisor with questions for fear you'll be incurring higher expenses. If your sole investment portfolio is your employer's retirement plan, and you do not have debt problems or complex estate issues (such as children from two marriages), you are probably best served by the hourly arrangement. As one possible resource for hourly advice, look into the Garrett Planning Network; it's a network of financial planners who work exclusively on an hourly basis and are focused on a middle-income clientele. You can visit their site at www.garrettplanningnetwork.com.

But note that there is no regulation governing the term "fee-only," so anyone can use it, regardless of whether it is accurate. A directory of fee-only advisors who have been vetted can be found at www.napfa.org, the site of the National Association of Personal Financial Advisors.

Trust Companies

Some of the largest financial firms in the country are trust companies. If you are dealing with a trust officer of a trust company, there is no question that you are dealing with a fiduciary.

Trust companies often require a minimum account size, or at least a minimum annual fee, which would be justified only on accounts of a certain size or larger.

In trust companies, there is a fiduciary duty to clients and/or to the client's trust documents, and this is of paramount importance. Some clients find the corporate structure and size of a trust company reassuring, while others find these companies to be too rules-bound and too concerned about their own liability. If you are considering using a trust company, it's a good idea to interview at least three of different sizes. Ask for references (they will need to secure clients' permissions first), call the references, and ask what the companies are like and what should be changed about them, and ask about the individual trust officers they use.

Registered Investment Advisors (RIAs)

As mentioned previously, RIAs are regulated according to the Investment Company Act of 1940, which includes their legal requirement to always act in the best interests of the client. Anyone who gives investment advice must register either with every state where more than five clients are located (with the exception of a few states that require registration for only one client), or, if they manage more than $100 million in other people's money, with the Securities and Exchange Commission (the SEC).

Ideally the RIA's clients' investments will be kept ("custodied") at a third-party firm, such as Fidelity, TD Ameritrade, Vanguard, Schwab, or others. One red flag to watch for: Ponzi schemers will have their own custody firms, which enable them to send out falsified statements. Be extra cautious of independent firms that do not custody with a third party.

Pushback Possibilities

In the back of this book, you'll find the Fiduciary Oath of the National Association of Personal Financial Advisors (NAPFA), which you can ask your advisor to sign. You can also download it for free from www.napfa.org. If the advisor does not agree to sign it, you may hear, as the justification, one of these statements:

1. I do not need to be held to a fiduciary standard because I always act in the best interests of my clients.

2. The regulatory burden is already onerous, and if I had to comply with every single little detail of a fiduciary standard, I would go out of business with paperwork and red tape.

3. When I am doing financial planning, I do act in a fiduciary capacity. The investment recommendations I make are incidental to the financial planning process, so a fiduciary standard is not appropriate. I am only giving guidance. It is up to the clients to make their own decisions. Buyer beware is just the way the industry works.

4. I provide full written disclosure for all my clients. That is enough to satisfy my fiduciary obligation. If clients don't read what I send them, then that's their problem.

(Would you agree that investment recommendations are "incidental" to a financial plan?)

As noted in a June 19, 2009, MSN Money column by Liz Pulliam Weston, "Can You Trust Your Adviser?," Barbara Roper, director of investor protection for the Consumer Federation of America, said, "How are people supposed to understand that the person who was their trusted advisor has now turned into a salesperson who no longer has to have their best interests at heart? There's no way you can disclose away that confusion."

There are tens of thousands of fiduciary-based RIAs who manage to make a decent living, do good work, live good lives, and pass their government compliance audits. It is worth asking why a professional would not arrange his or her business model to be legally held to the same fiduciary standard.

TEST 3: Works Transparently

Costs, Compensation, and Conflicts

There is an unusual amount of resistance in the financial community to disclosing the total compensation an advisor receives for his or her advice.

In 2009, a panel report published by the CFA (Chartered Financial Analyst) Institute, "U.S. Financial Regulatory Reform: The Investors' Perspective," stated:

> "Meanwhile, although investors are encouraged to place their trust in 'investment advisors,' compensation practices in the industry are riddled with conflicts of interest that may encourage sales of products that are not in clients' best interests. The disclosures that investors are supposed to rely on in making investment decisions are often inadequate and overly complex and typically arrive after the sale—long past the point when they could have been useful to investors analyzing their investment options."[7]

A 2009 report by the Rand Corporation found that more than half of consumer-investors believed they paid nothing for the advice they received. Rarely is this actually the case, and certainly not for more than half of the investing public! Otherwise the financial industry would not exist.

It can be difficult to realize that just because compensation has never been discussed or disclosed doesn't mean that it doesn't exist. It can also be distressing to discover that where you thought you had a friendship, you actually had a non-disclosed business relationship.

A False Friendship

As tax time approached in early 2011, Jack and Constance tried to get compensation information from their former commission-and-fee broker so they could deduct her fees for 2010 on their Schedule A. The broker had never told them that her fees were deductible. And, in fact, they had decided to fire her a few months earlier when they discovered that what they thought was a friendship (the broker's invitations to go shopping, go to concerts, have dinner at her house) was actually a non-disclosed business relationship. They were hurt. Adding insult to injury, because she had not told them about the deductible fees, they had missed out on more than $100,000 in tax deductions over the decade of their relationship.

As April 15 approached, here is how the former broker replied to their request for her 2010 fees and a 1099-R:

"I do not know the answer to either of your questions."

Her answer was probably not a lie, although getting the answer might have been as simple as making a phone call or two. But its curtness conveyed the underlying message.

When asked directly by the accountant instead of by Jack and Constance, the broker countered (stunningly) with this:

"I would be happy to do the research needed to provide you with this information…however, it will take me about an hour. My business model does not afford me the luxury of doing free work for former or non-clients. I would suggest that [Constance] either ask her 'fee only' financial planner to figure it out, or she can hire me to do the tax research."

Tax research. Research to reveal to her former clients, who thought she was a friend, how much the broker had made on their account in the prior year. The figure was a little over $12,000 just for that single year.

One could ask: How much is friendship worth in the financial world?

So what can be done to obtain full disclosure of total costs? Demand for transparency would be a good start. Ask professionals to complete a Compensation Disclosure Form like the one in the back of this book (reprints can be ordered through the National Association of Personal Financial Advisors at 847-483-5400) every time you receive advice, and every time you sign up for a product, program, or plan. Also check the ADV, the disclosure form filed with the adviser's regulator and required to be given to you.

Costs: Visible and Invisible

As Jack and Constance found, sometimes what you are paying for advice or products is clear, and sometimes it's buried in the paperwork. You are then left to wonder, are you paying a lot for this solution, or a little? How do you compare the benefit to the cost? Do you have this solution because it was the best thing for your unique situation, or for someone else's (your broker's) benefit? What if the peace of mind you paid for is only temporary?

Research shows that our brains tolerate paying for things in percentages more readily than in flat dollar amounts. (Which would you rather pay to a realtor for selling your $450,000 home: 6%, or $27,000?) If mutual funds, separate account managers, financial product manufacturers, and brokers charged transparent, flat dollar fees we could see for every transaction, we might not so readily invest. But because most charges are shown as a percentage of the account value or are hidden in the cost of a share price, the pain of paying them is numbed.

Through your background checks and the ADV, you can determine whether an advisor claiming to be fee-only also sells insurance products; works for a securities broker-dealer; is a registered representative; or has a fee-sharing arrangement with the person who referred you. However, it also helps to understand which costs and compensation will or will not be readily apparent.

Here's an example: The Megabucks Super Sector Special Small Cap Fund (ticker MBSSSX) charges a 3% load and 1% as a management fee. It is just one product manufactured by Megabucks Funds, the parent company. MBSSSX pays a distribution fee (a "trailer") of up to .25% to brokers. If the brokerage firm, James & Juniper, buys $24,000 of MBSSSX in your wrap account, you actually invest $23,280 ($24,000 minus 3% load). In the first year, you pay a wrap fee to J&J of 1% ($232.80), a load of 3% ($720.00), the fund's internal fee of 1% ($232.80), plus (your share price gets hit by) the trailer of .25% x $23,280, or $58.20 per year. In the first year, the financial industry has collected $1243.80 on your $24,000 purchase. To do better than staying even in the first 12 months, MBSSSX must return at least 5.3%. While all of these costs are disclosed in prospectuses and some can be found on statements, most investors don't read prospectuses and don't understand their statements, so the costs might as well be invisible.

There are visible and invisible costs of investing that vary according to the type of professional and the kind of investment product:

1. If you do it yourself, purchasing investments in a retail investment account:

   a. For individual stocks, exchange-traded funds and bonds

   Visible: Commissions on stock and bond trades range from $2.50 to several hundred dollars, depending on brokerage firm, transaction size, and number of transactions.

   Invisible: None.

   b. For mutual funds

   Visible: Loads of 0% to 5% to purchase and/or sell. Loads depend upon share class. Share classes often go by letters such as A, B, or C class, but sometimes have names, such as Admiral.

   Invisible: Internal management fees range from .15% to 3.0% charged against the total fund value, which in turn affects the per-share value of the fund. Ron Rhoades, professor at Alfred State University, and co-author of **The Art and Science of Investing**, estimates that between markups, trading fees, bid-ask spreads, record-keeping costs, and fees to use the no-transaction-fee platforms of brokerage firms, total costs to mutual fund shareholders can approach 3.0% per year inside most funds.

2. If you hire a commission-and-fee manager who selects investments:

   a. For wrap accounts (where the professional selects a collection of mutual funds)

   Visible: AUM fee from .5% to 2.5% of the account value

Invisible: Advisor receives 50% to 100% of the wrap fee, plus may also receive commission-like fees from the mutual fund companies (called "trailers"), and part of the load, if any. Advisor may have quotas to fill on certain mutual funds. Add other costs detailed above under "mutual funds." Advisor's firm may have revenue sharing arrangements.

Revenue Sharing Arrangements

Blaine Aikin, CEO of fiduciary360, in an interview with **Inside Information** publisher Bob Veres, discussed his former role as head of product development for a national brokerage firm: "Whenever you're creating a product for the suitability side, all of a sudden you have to be competitive in two respects: as an investment, and also to attract people to sell it. You have to build enough compensation into the expense so that brokers and people who work under the suitability standard will be motivated to sell it."

Veres points out that this creates incentives counter to the consumer's best interests. "If you can pay a little bit more than the next guy," Aikin explains, "then you have an obvious advantage. This creates actual competition for everybody to put more expense on there. Somebody else adds a little bit of a bonus commission, so you have to match them and maybe do a little more, and somebody else matches that and does a little more, and every time there is another hike in costs, the consumer is basically paying for that distribution arms race out of his own pocket."

b. For Separately Managed Accounts (SMAs)

Visible: AUM fee from 1.0% to 3.0% of the account value, plus trading costs of 5 cents to 15 cents per share.

Invisible: Advisor personally gets 25% to 75% of the fee. Advisor may or may not get compensation and perks (travel, meals, software, gifts) from separate account wholesalers. Firm may or may not receive revenue sharing arrangements.

c. For insurance or annuity products

Visible: Premium payments.

Invisible: Commissions range from 10% to 90% of the first year's premium on an insurance policy, and from 1% to 11% of the total invested in an annuity. For a rough guess of the commission on a variable annuity, figure 1% of commission for each year in the surrender period (example: a 7-year surrender period = 7% commission). Ongoing management fees of underlying investment funds are from .2% to 3.0%.

Mortality expenses: .2% to .6%

Administration fees: .2% to 1.0%

Total: Many insurance and annuity products, in particular variable annuities, have total annual fees and costs ranging between 2% and 4% of the amount invested.

d. For individual bonds

Visible: AUM fee from .25% to 3.0% based upon cost of bonds. Trading costs range from $6 to $50.

Invisible: Difference between broker's wholesale cost and retail price is charged (the "markup"). Markup can range from 0% to 10% of bond value. Advisor personally receives 25% to 100% of AUM fee. If commission, broker receives none to very little of trading costs, and 20% to 100% of markup.

Soft Dollars, Welcome to the Financial Supermarket

Supermarket shelf placement is essential to the success of brands like Proctor & Gamble. Having a product at shoppers' eye-level has been confirmed by shopper studies to increase sales. If you make children's cereal, for example, you want your box with your TV ad's cartoon character on the lower shelf. If you make anti-wrinkle cream, you want it to be 5 feet 4 inches off the floor. And if you make size 12 shoe inserts, the top shelf will do just fine.

You may be surprised to learn that many product purveyors pay the supermarket to place their product on a particular spot on the shelf. Essentially the purveyor rents the shelf space and restocks the product, saving the grocery store the labor. And purveyors bid against each other for the best shelf spots! So the grocery store is both their landlord and their customer.

Savvy grocery shoppers scan from the top shelf down to the bottom for lower priced products that accomplish similar things to the higher priced products but haven't bid for shelf placements.

Imagine a brokerage firm as a financial supermarket. And instead of shopping yourself, you employ a professional to go shopping for you. Do you want a professional who can go into any supermarket, or a professional who can only shop at one store? Do you want a professional who looks for products only at eye-level, where the pay-to-play products are, or one who will scan the top and bottom shelves for the very best and most cost-effective product for your money? What if some of the products that would be best for you are not even in the supermarket? Would you like to know if your professional would even consider these?

Investment product manufacturers are often not directly paying the professional to recommend their product, but might be inviting him or her and a spouse to "educational" conferences at spa-and-golf resorts, for example. If you were an avid reader of the financial news in 2008-2009, you might remember the phrase "soft dollars." Soft dollars refers essentially to pay-to-play, when money is not the explicit medium of exchange; instead there is free technology, spa days at a conference, free continuing education credits, or allowances for a higher commission schedule for trades at that firm. Soft dollars, like revenue sharing payments, drive up costs.

3. If you hire a fee-only professional:

    a. Account with a third party custodian (see discussion below on Custodians)

    Visible: Can be paid by AUM, flat fee, or hourly fee. AUM fees generally range from .5% to 2.0% of the account value. Annual flat fees can range anywhere from $1,500 to $25,000. Hourly fees range from $50 to $350. May have trading costs charged by custodian of less than $1.00 to $100 per trade depending upon security type.

    Invisible: If selecting mutual funds, see "Mutual Funds" above. Otherwise, none.

    b. Trust Company/Private Banking Account

    Visible: Management fees of .75% to 1.75%, plus trading costs of 5 cents to 15 cents per share.

Invisible: In general, none. Portfolio manager receives salary plus bonus based upon performance of selected anonymous accounts. Trust officer is salaried plus gets a bonus usually based upon number and size of client accounts. Private banker may have quotas to fill on products and receive bonuses accordingly.

Other Invisible Costs

Referral Fees

Understanding how a financial advisor "plays in the sandbox" with other professionals can provide a clue to his or her potential conflicts of interest. If the advisor will pay other professionals, such as accountants, to refer clients, then was that advisor endorsed by the accountant out of self-interest or your interest? Conversely, if the advisor accepts referral fees from accountants, lawyers, insurance agents, or bankers for sending clients, then your best interests could be compromised when the referrals go the other way, too.

Some professionals have office-sharing arrangements with a lawyer, a financial planner, an insurance agent, and/or an accountant in the same building. They may be together because they are referring clients to each other. Perhaps they've gone so far as to purchase the building as partners. If a group of professionals find that they work well together, then there may be great synergy and benefits to the client in pooling resources and/or forming a formal or informal alliance. It helps for a supporting cast of professionals to communicate frequently. However, if there are cross-referrals, rent-offsets, staff sharing, computer sharing, or profit sharing agreements among them, these should be fully disclosed to you, verbally and in writing.

Custodians: The Company an Advisor Keeps

The place where your money is actually housed (the firm whose name is on your statements) is known as the custodian. Many people confuse the importance of picking the right custodian with the importance of picking the right professional. The custodian, in general, has very little to do with the quality of customized advice you will receive. For most custodians, the advisor is the primary client, not the investor. Why? The advisor controls a large pool of assets. One investor's account is a few drops in the pool.

Nevertheless, a lot can be read into the choice an advisor makes for a custodian for his or her clients' money. We would like to think an advisor chooses a firm based upon what works best for the clients. In fact, the decision may be based upon several factors, such as: how trading technology makes the advisor's job easier or more lucrative; whether the custodian offers back-office sales and/or operations support; the custodian's tools for administering and/or selling 401(k)s; participation in private equity funds, oil-and-gas partnerships or real estate trusts; seminars-in-a-box for attracting new clients; bond desk inventory and capabilities; banking availability; a bonus paid annually for staying with that firm; and commission sharing. Certain firms specialize in or offer some of these. None do all of them or do all of them well. It would be important to know what aspects of a firm were most important in the advisor's custodian decision.

For example, a fee-only advisor signs with a particular firm in order to provide an options service for his clients, but he is extremely discouraged with the firm's record-keeping and statements. Although he helps his clients avoid hundreds of thousands of dollars in losses in the 2008 downturn by using the options service, the clients still complain about the quality of the statements. So now he is up-front with new clients and tells them that until another custodian firm opens up to options, they will need to tolerate this custodian and its poor administrative quality for the sake of participating in the options service.

Ask your potential advisor why he or she has chosen a particular custodian. For some advisors, it will be because that firm offered them the most money to move their clients there, or that they are under a non-compete (with compensation) agreement not to go anywhere else. That is not the best answer, obviously, but many advisors may be honest enough to give it.

Others may claim it's the "technology," or the "culture," or the "bond desk." Ask them to elaborate on how that reason helps them help you.

Accurate, friendly administration and record-keeping from a custodian is equally as important as advisor competence and quality investment products. It is hard to overstate the aggravation and frustration caused by a firm's error in wrong addresses, wrong middle initials, wrong tax reporting, wrong cost basis accounting, and so on. And once you are in the custodian's system, it is cumbersome to move out again. Shoddy customer service from a custodian is a high but invisible cost.

Ask a potential advisor's references about any problems with administration, statements, accounting, support staff, or customer service representatives.

Unnecessary taxes

It is estimated that the lack of tax considerations in mutual funds ends up costing shareholders anywhere from 1.4% to 4.9% of their funds' assets per year. Along with mutual funds, most other investments have tax costs of some kind. A wrong move in the federal income tax arena can mean the difference between paying 15% and 43%, a 28% mistake. A wrong move in the estate tax arena, such as poor choices in prioritizing which accounts to leave in the estate, can mean a 45%

or even an 80% mistake. Avoiding 28% and 80% mistakes is one way investment professionals should earn their fees.

Ask what kind of tax planning the professional does. Ideally, the professional meets with clients in the fourth quarter of every year, and preferably with their accountants, too, to review what tax minimization strategies might be available before December 31.

Ask how the professional implements estate-planning advice. Ideally he or she will proactively coordinate with the estate planning attorney and accountant to prioritize income distributions, and retitle accounts and beneficiary designations if necessary.

Risk Mistakes

While big tax mistakes can be a good reason to doubt the competence of your financial advisor, there are usually two sides to every risk story. When a single investment loses money, we tend to judge poorly the professional who chose the investment. As we have seen in Chapter 5, it is normal to expect that investments will go up and down. Losses in value can be concerning, or they can be an opportunity to buy more. It is important to remain on plan within your asset allocation, even in the face of losses. (Remember, rebalance regardless regularly!)

Remember too that it is important to understand all of the risks of an investment before entering into it. Ask what the worst-case scenario is and its likelihood. Professionals should disclose all of the risks to you. No investment is risk-free.

The risk mistake can occur when we take unnecessary risk in the hope of achieving an outsized return. Every investment and portfolio has a risk-return ratio. Your goal should be to take the minimum risk necessary to maximize your odds of success. Anything else can become an invisible cost.

As we will see in Chapter 7, sometimes even the professionals get trapped by their own emotions and make irrational decisions about risk.

TEST 4: Has Done a Personal Financial Plan

Financial advisors are not immune from trying to avoid the hard work of defining goals in the financial lifestyle planning process. It's important to find a planner who does not just talk about lifestyle planning. The longer an advisor has had his or her own financial lifestyle plan, the better it is for you. The experienced advisor will be far better at seeing how a plan evolves over time and can succeed with thought and care.

A financial planner who has done a lifestyle plan for him- or herself will also have experienced the emotional biases, money messages, and decisions that go into making a plan. These advisors will already recognize that they can't avoid the kinds of emotional obstacles we will cover in the next chapter; they are aware of them, will work hard to control and mitigate them, and to manage around them.

Bear in mind too, that if, for example, you view the sharing of money as a way of showing you care for others, your planner should have experience and clear thinking about his or her own sharing decisions. Financial planners who understand their own messages and beliefs will be best suited to understand yours.

TEST 5: Addresses Your Plan Comprehensively

Many financial professionals are not comfortable asking you about your money history, or about your will, or your plan for old age. So they leave those questions out.

This is no better than a primary care doctor who is not comfortable asking you about your bowel habits or your sex life. As part of a planner's job of thinking comprehensively, he or she has to ask uncomfortable questions. For many people, a visit to the financial planner is like rolling a trip to the dentist, a session in math class, and an hour of psychotherapy into one meeting. A planner who cares will use tact and thought before delving into a potentially sensitive topic with you. Also, he or she will not use esoteric financial jargon, nor will there be a gatekeeper or constant voicemail when you call.

Hire a planner who will keep you accountable and on track. Good financial planners are like good coaches whose chief concern is not for themselves but for their athletes—and for their continuing progress. Good planners do not just ask about what you have. They want to know who you are.

Your Part

As we've already seen, old financial flashpoints or money messages can make us anxious when certain money issues arise. Anything a planner asks or says that increases your stress or fear may indicate that you will be unable to receive his or her advice. You can avoid this and help the planner do an increasingly better job by letting him or her know when you are uncomfortable in any way. You don't have to understand or explain why; you simply need to recognize your own emotional state when you're not being mindful.

If you have discovered some topic areas that might cause emotional upset, make your planner aware of these so he or she can stop and listen to your concerns. One natural tendency we all have is to sit and nod as if we understand, even when we don't. Instead, ask your planner to back up and review, or slow down and re-explain anything you did not fully hear and understand. It is also your job to be as cooperative as possible in letting your planner get to know you. Without this, there is the risk of misunderstandings later. A long-lasting, mutually beneficial relationship is always a two-way street.

What if you have to fire your advisor?

For some people, leaving a professional advisor is as simple as saying goodbye, understanding that the advisor has not been acting in their best interests. For others, it's tougher: there is sensitivity about possibly hurting the advisor's feelings, or an unwillingness to be accusatory. Many of us are not cut out for conflict, and we avoid difficult conversations, even at our own peril.

If you are a person who has trouble figuring out what to say or how to say it when the relationship with an advisor goes sour, my experience has been that it's better to allow yourself some time to get used to the idea that the professional relationship should end. You could discuss with a trusted friend or associate how you see your financial life unfolding, or even begin meeting with your newly chosen advisor.

With time, the right approach for ending a relationship with an advisor will come to you. If you need ideas, here are a few that might work:

- It's about the business model: "I've decided I want to work with someone who is legally bound to a fiduciary duty to manage my finances."
- It's about the industry: "I've decided not to use insurance companies/broker-dealers/trust companies/registered investment advisors any longer for my investment needs."
- It's a family matter: "My spouse/parent/child/sibling has introduced me to a professional that they really like and we have decided to go with that person."
- It's geography: "I've decided to work only with local people," or "I have decided against working with local people."

It is not necessary to explain to the advisor that you felt he or she did not listen, did not care, or did not put your best interests first, if saying so would make you uncomfortable (even if it was the truth).

However, if you believe that your advisor is guilty of misconduct or a possibly illegal action, you should promptly notify your state regulator—plus the company's comptroller and/or department of financial services—and seek legal counsel.

Notes:

1. Page 107: Mary Pilon and Jason Zweig, "Who's Advising Your Adviser?" *The Wall Street Journal*, November 20-21, 2010, p. B8.

2. Page 111: Jeff Daniher, National Association of Personal Financial Advisors discussion board, November 2009. Used with permission.

3. Page 113: Staff of the U.S. Securities and Exchange Commission, "Study on Investment Advisers and Broker-Dealers: As Required by Section 913 of the Dodd-Frank Wall Street Reform and Consumer Protection Act," January 2011.

4. Page 113: Financial Industry Regulatory Authority, About page, on the Internet at www.finra.gov/About (visited August 8, 2013).

5. Page 113: Bureau of Labor Statistics, U.S. Department of Labor, **Occupational Outlook Handbook**, 2012-13 Edition, Insurance Sales Agents, on the Internet at http://www.bls.gov/ooh/sales/insurance-sales-agents.htm (visited August 08, 2013).

6. Page 114: "U.S. Financial Regulatory Reform: The Investors' Perspective," A Report by the Investors' Working Group, An Independent Taskforce Sponsored by CFA Institute Centre for Financial Market Integrity and Council of Institutional Investors, July 2009, page 15.

7. Page 124: Ibid

7

Emotional Threats to Mindfulness

"Emotion is the enemy of sound investment."
~Donald Ratajczak, economist

Once you and your planner have created a financial lifestyle plan that reflects your values and goals, it's time to put that plan into action. And just as you do, you'll encounter challenges. Some of these will be fallout from those persistent old money messages; others may arise simply because we are human and our minds work in certain predictable ways.

When we make an investing decision, what sometimes looks and sounds like reasoning is actually rationalizing. We have to be mindful about understanding when emotions are hijacking reason. The object of this chapter is to explore how our brains work when it comes to assessing risk, look at the common errors we make systematically, and learn how to recognize and overcome common emotional obstacles.

Nature versus Nurture in Risk Behavior

Just like our tendencies to eat too much, lean the wrong way on our skis, and flinch just before we pull a trigger, we all make systematic errors in judgment that often prevent rational decisions. In the field of psychology these errors are called "biases," and they are often rooted in emotion.[1] They can be overcome, first by awareness and then through practicing new ways of thinking and acting—sort of like learning to eat sensibly, leaning down the hill on our skis, and controlling our reflexes. After a lot of practice, we can develop entirely new mental habits.

Behavioral Economics and Psychology

The "invisible hand" concept is taught in basic economics. Espoused in the 18th century by Adam Smith, the "father of economics," it describes how, in a free market, our innate sense of profit maximization will lead to decisions that allocate resources—land, labor, and capital—in ways that make the highest and best use of them.

In the 20th century, some economists began to question, in a scientific way, the assumption that actors in an economy always behave according to Smith's assumption of profit maximization—that is, sometimes they behave counter to it, which isn't rational.

For example, how would the "invisible hand" explain charitable acts? Most charitable acts do not result in maximizing profit for the donor; purely economically speaking, charity is quite the opposite. Another example: why do people want to buy just about anything at a discount except stocks? Why do many people sell stocks when they go down in value, but sell everything else when it goes up? What could be the reason for such irrational economic decisions?

Behavioral economists were not satisfied to assume that economic interactions are conducted by two rational parties, devoid of emotion. Since the 1970s, their experiments have shown that, unbeknownst to us, there are many more emotions guiding our actions than Adam Smith might have believed.

Two Decision-making Engines

Imagine your brain as two engines, an Emotional Engine and a Rational Engine, which drive your decision-making.

The Emotional Engine is the first part of the brain to react to a decision. Also known as the limbic system or "Reptile Brain," it is unconscious, automatic, rapid, impulsive, passionate, unaware, specific, social, and personalized. It is pure emotional essence, focused solely on the moment. Because it is unconscious, we are often not aware we are using it.

The Rational Engine, also known as "Einstein brain," or the neocortex, is slow, conscious, patient, planning-focused, deliberate, cold, controlled, deductive, self-aware, neutral, asocial, and depersonalized. It is purely rational, but focused on the lessons of the past and projections into the future. Most importantly, it naturally assumes it has the Emotional Engine under control.

When you become a sports champion, practice emergency room medicine, fly airplanes, or become desensitized to anything that would normally trigger emotion (like competing for a championship, dealing with blood and guts, or experiencing engine failure), you learn to suppress the quick responsiveness of the Emotional Engine and engage your Rational Engine in judgment and decision-making. If star athletes, doctors, and pilots did not practice this, emotions would rule their decisions, with disastrous results.

However, we would not want to be completely ruled by our Rational Engines. Psychologists call emotions the "lubricants of reason." Patients who have a congenital disconnection with their Emotional Engine show extreme difficulty making simple decisions, such as setting a calendar appointment.

Physiologically, the Emotional Engine includes our brainstem and cerebellum, which monitor and maintain our bodily functions. The Emotional Engine's singular focus is survival. This part of the brain is terrible at forethought and planning. It generates the fight-or-flight response, so it is very good at making sure we breathe, bite things, run away, or freeze like a deer in the headlights. It is the oldest part of our brains. Demonstrating how powerfully it manages its own survival, it is typically the last part of our body to die. Because the Emotional Engine also includes the amygdala, hypothalamus, and hippocampus, it controls the release of hormones and creates, stores, and retrieves memories. It learns best from intensely emotional experiences.

The Rational Engine, the neocortex, was the last part of the brain to evolve. It is where "you" are generated—your thoughts, dreams, hopes, and goals. It is the analytical part of the brain that weighs the pros and cons of possible actions. When it comes to making financial decisions, the Rational Engine can be thought of as our human resource. Often the Emotional Engine, when it comes to financial decisions, is a human liability.

The Rational Engine believes it is the one in control. However, the Emotional Engine consumes 98% of the brain's energy. Part of the Emotional Engine has its own circuitry that can operate independent of the Rational Engine; but without the Emotional Engine, the Rational Engine shuts down.

Imagine that between the Rational Engine and the Emotional Engine, there is a trapdoor that slams shut when stressed. Inside the Emotional Engine, there is a lot of free-flowing information, allowing four *billion* bits per second of data to be processed. When open, the drawbridge only allows two *million* bits per second to reach the Rational Engine. The open state of the drawbridge is the only state in which we can be mindful.

Because of the five-to-one difference in nerve synapses between the two areas, the Rational Engine has less influence on our thinking and is slower to respond. In twelve milliseconds, your Emotional Engine has processed what will take your Rational Engine another twenty-eight milliseconds to register. In some cases, that's too late. The drawbridge was shut twenty-eight milliseconds ago and anxiety, fear, excitement, and/or greed have taken over.

Emotions will trigger either a "danger" or a "reward" response. To the Emotional Engine, there is no middle ground. If you are worried, your reward system shuts down and cannot enjoy anything pleasurable. If you are excited, it is going to be tougher to get you worried and into "danger" mode.

You may have experienced this when you thought about a momentarily tense situation and wondered, "Why did I do that?" Danger or reward responses took over before your Rational Engine could process the situation. Here's an everyday example: We fail to notice a red light turning green, so when the driver behind us honks, our initial reaction might be anger or irritation, before we realize milliseconds later that we made a mistake and it's time to go forward. If this has happened to you, then you can appreciate how quickly the Emotional Engine acts compared to the delay in the Rational Engine's reaction.

When we are in a highly emotional state, our Emotional Engines do not take time to think things out. This evolution tends to serve us well when our survival is threatened, but works against us in the money world, where patience, rationality, and higher-than-primate intelligence are often required.

Despite our best intentions to not "be emotional," we all have emotional reactions that prevent us from making rational decisions, particularly involving financial risk.

The Strength of Tribal Bonds

Even though it may seem that we are rarely in situations where our actual survival is threatened, a little further analysis reveals why the Emotional Engine doesn't agree. In ancient times, survival depended on being part of a tribe. In modern times, we still have groups of people with whom we identify and feel we belong to. The Emotional Engine fears expulsion from the tribe. Not only is it embarrassing, but prehistorically it's linked to life and death.

Expulsion from the tribe, to our Emotional Engine, can mean the loss of a lifestyle to which we have become accustomed, or a loss of status in the eyes of those close to us. A client once told me that if she did not maintain her shopping budget, she would not be able to hang out with her friends. She was serious. The prospect of saying, "I'm out," on the next shopping trip was too painful for her to contemplate.

I was riding the ski lift once with a dentist friend who was close to 70 years old. He told me that he had sold his practice, but the new owners were glad to pay him to work as much or as little as he wanted. His circle of friends had originated from his sailing, flying, and snow-skiing hobbies, which he still enjoyed. So in order to continue to afford these leisure activities—and the friends who shared them—he had to continue working longer than he had wished. Although he received a lot of fulfillment from treating his dental patients, he confessed that all of his hobbies were expensive and if he could just find one that wasn't, he could scale back his work hours and have more leisure time. He didn't know what to do. It was clear he did not want to leave his tribes.

Any threat to our perceived placement in our tribe feels to our Emotional Engine like a threat to our survival. That primal fear, justified or not, is what we need to be equipped to handle when we open investment statements, reach for a credit card, or listen to a financial advisor.

Biases: Rational versus Stupid

The problem is, many times we do not know that the mistake we are making is irrational until after we have made it. All along, we think we are being rational and intelligent. Our Rational Engine thinks it is in charge, but the Emotional Engine gets the best of us. As mentioned previously, when we make judgment errors systematically, the errors are called, in academic psychological terms, "biases." Biases in this sense are not related to prejudice. They are more related to errors of intuition. If I could banish one word from clients' vocabularies, it would be "stupid." Most of the time, they use this term about a decision they later regret, recognizing that it was based on an emotion—fear, greed, anxiety, or excitement. Succumbing to an emotion-based bias is not stupid if you are not aware of its power over you. It is simply human.

By understanding the ways in which your Emotional Engine can sabotage rational decision-making, you can be prepared to either make better investing decisions yourself or make a better hiring decision about a professional. The first step to stop feeling stupid is to start getting smart about your biases!

In this chapter, we look at a collection of well-documented biases that apply to investing decisions. Sometimes we experience biases in combination, so complex emotions or behaviors can be explained by more than one bias. Give some thought to whether you have experienced these in the past, so that you can watch out for them in the future.

The Four Ms of the Emotional Engine

Biases, for our purposes, can be divided into four different areas:

1. Mental Defaults
2. Media-influenced Mistakes

3. Mathematical Errors

4. Manipulative Biases

1. Mental Defaults

Almost everyone is subject to mental defaults, or automatic reactions, and these are the most difficult reactions for the Rational Engine to counteract. The best we can do is be aware of them and try to avoid situations where they might enter into our decision-making. Let's look at some of the most common.

Loss Aversion

The following two-part question gets at your preferences.

Part 1 of 2: Which would you prefer, A or B?

A. Gaining a sure $3000

B. Having an 80% chance of gaining $4000 with a 20% chance of gaining nothing

Part 2 of 2: Which would you prefer, C or D?

C. Losing a total of $3000

D. Having an 80% chance of losing $4000 with a 20% chance of losing nothing

In a widely-cited study by Nobel-prize winning psychologists Daniel Kahneman and Amos Tversky, published in *American Psychologist* in April 1984, most people chose the equivalent of A and D. They would take the sure win in A and the 20% chance of losing nothing in D.

Mathematically, however, you're really better off with choices B and C. You multiply the probability by the amount in question, as follows:

A. 100% x $3000 = $3000

B. (80% x $4000) + (20% x $0) = $3200

C. 100% x (-$3000) = -$3000

D. (80% x (-$4000)) + (20% x $0) = -$3200

We tend to think that most people make choices to avoid risk. However, the study showed that most people are actually loss averse, not risk averse: Choice D is more risky than Choice C, indicating that we will take more risk to avoid loss.[2]

Risk aversion essentially means a preference for certainty over uncertainty. Choices A and D don't express this preference. We are risk averse (although mathematically wrong) when we choose A in the first question, but risk seeking (and thus loss averse) when we choose D in the second question.

Investment losses, to most people, come with the pain of regret, which has been shown to hurt as much as the pain of grief. We have a powerful incentive not to recognize losses, even when doing so is in our best interests. Loss aversion encourages us to delay the pain, hide it if possible, or try to stretch it out over a longer period of time. This unfortunately compounds its effects.

For those who inherit investments, loss aversion hits twice: once when we lose a loved one, and again when we sell something he or she has owned. Five years after the death of my father, I still had some investments he purchased that did not fit into my asset allocation. This waiting allowed me to delay the feeling of loss again. I admit it has been far easier (though not very mindful) for me to advise clients to sell their inherited securities than it has been to do this myself.

In an early 2000s study, Keith Chen, associate professor of economics at Yale University, found that capuchin monkeys showed a preference for holding on to food they already had, instead of risking a coin toss that could have given them more food half the time and no food the other half of the time. In other words, they would not choose to flip a coin to get more food, if it meant an equal chance of losing the food they already had. Chen suggests this is a clue to how hard-wired we are to avoid loss and regret.

Keeping all holdings in cash or savings accounts instead of investing them in stocks and bonds is an example of this risk averse hard-wiring; we do it to over-insure against loss. But the over-insurance "premium" is actually the difference between the inflation rate and the interest rate on our cash. We're losing purchasing power, but that is not a loss we tend to feel so acutely.

Endowment Effect

Loss aversion can apply to spending decisions, too. As we saw in Chapter 4, it's tempting to become overly attached to things we own. Behavioral economists call this the "endowment effect."

The endowment effect is stronger with items we have and use, like houses, boats, and cars, than for things we simply hold to sell. It is as if we have a mental bucket in which to keep things-I-will-sell-someday-but-use-for-myself-in-the-meantime (houses, cars, or art, for example) and another bucket for things-I-am-only-holding-to-make-a-profit-on (stocks, rental real estate, tradable collectibles, for example). We attach a higher price to things we have other uses for than simply trading. So when you're ready to sell the first kind of asset (your first home, for example), ask yourself what you would pay for it if you didn't already own it. That number will normally be much lower than the sales price you would pick otherwise. Use that as your reference point for an asking price, otherwise the endowment effect will cause you to ask more than the market will bear.

Successful entrepreneurs and investors are known for resisting the pull of loss aversion. Losses in their view are part of being successful over the long term and they move on easily from them.

Be wary of advisors who are unaware of loss aversion. Advisors whose only goal for the money they manage is "more," or who promise perpetually positive returns, do not have a realistic view about loss. Market cycles and losses in value will occur with almost every investment at some point (although rarely all at once), so if there is no mindful, rational plan for them, you and your advisor will both be in trouble.

Substitution

When we are trying to make a decision but don't have the facts we need, our Emotional Engine will automatically substitute an easier-to-deal-with question instead and we'll rely on the answer we give to it. The question is an emotional one, and it might go something like this, in this fairly common investing example: Instead of reading the fine print on a prospectus (the document detailing the structure and risks of the investment), or having an attorney or personal CFO read it for us, we might simply ask ourselves, "Do I feel okay about the person/company who is suggesting this investment to me?" If we trust the person, if we like them or think they are intelligent and competent, then we figure the investment must be a good idea.

Studies show that few people read prospectuses and contracts, even after the SEC ruled that they must be written in plain English. In fact, in the majority of cases, the prospectus is mailed *after* the investment purchase has been made. If you have ever regretted a large investment purchase decision, chances are that it'll only cross your mind much later that you didn't read the documents. Suppose that you had initially read that an increase in the price of crude oil was a risk to consider? Or that if the value of the dollar fell, your investment could be wiped out? Or that your principal would be subject to large surrender charges for up to 11 years?

Many professionals do not disclose the fine print in an investment for one of two possible reasons. The first is that the lawyers who write the prospectuses and contracts are trying to cover the bases, so if the professional disclosed every single risk of every single investment outlined in the prospectus, this would be like the doctor telling the patient every single risk of surgery in extreme detail and in medical jargon before going forward. Too much information, sometimes, is actually not in the customer's best interests.

The second possible reason is that the professional him- or herself has not read the prospectus and so does not know all of the risks involved in the investment. And this goes for any type of investment, although insurance contracts tend to be common sources of substitution.

In the same way that clients believe their representatives would disclose risks to them, the representatives believe the financial companies would do the same. With some financial products, the benefits sound so compelling that neither party really wants to hear about the risks. After all, with advertised returns of 6% in an environment of sub-1% bank accounts, who cares what the risks or catches are?

Variable Annuities (VAs)

Every month, attorneys meet with thousands of people who want to exit a variable annuity. Of all the specific products that could be regulated, equity-indexed VAs are the ones garnering the most attention from state insurance commissioners. Three areas of annuities tend to be glossed over, or perhaps just forgotten, by either the selling agent or the client: surrender charges, internal fees, and guaranteed income riders. These three are explained below.

Some VAs have surrender charges (extra costs for surrendering the policy) that never go away, although the typical surrender charge period is about seven years. The surrender charge, which usually declines about 1% per year, mostly represents the amortization of the agent's commission over the surrender charge period. A typical surrender charge schedule might look something like Year 1- 7%, Year 2 - 6%, Year 3 - 5%, Year 4 - 4%, Year 5 - 3%, Year 6 - 2%, Year 7 - 1%. This means if the policy is surrendered in Year 1, the client is charged 7%. Most likely this also means the agent has earned a commission on the sale of approximately 7%. If the insurance company allowed investors to exit before they made back the commission produced by their profit on the annuity, they could lose money on the contract.

Because a VA is an insurance product, it comes with mortality and administration expenses that reduce the contract's value, in addition to the normal investment fees described in Chapter 6.

VAs are often sold with a guaranteed income feature, which appears as a rider on the policy: the eventual annuitization (income stream) from the initial investment will be based upon a principal amount that grows by a "guaranteed" percentage each year. But this is not the same as assuring a guaranteed return on your principal. Normally there is an additional charge for the rider that comes out of the annuity's value.

At a 2010 conference, David Jacobs, Ph.D., CFP®, of Pathfinder Financial Services, LLC, in Kailua, Hawaii, presented his analysis of variable annuity riders. After reading dozens of contracts, which can run to more than 100 pages, he deftly walked the audience through myriad problems these riders and the annuity products can cause for unsuspecting investors. He also quoted some startling statistics on how many of these contracts were being sold inappropriately.

At the end of the session, I asked him, "When you think about how many of these contracts are being sold, and the number of insurance agents it takes to sell them, can it really be that there are that many professionals who have no conscience? That would imply that a majority of annuities representatives sleep very well at night despite knowing that they are ripping people off. I find that hard to believe."

He corrected me, "It's not that they have no conscience. It's that they don't fully understand their own products and the available alternatives. The only education they get from the insurance companies is about the perks and benefits. The companies don't teach them the downsides and alternate methods of achieving the same objectives, so they actually believe they are providing great service and getting paid handsomely for it."

I added, "And that handsome payment gives them a nice incentive not to learn any more than they have to about it?" He just nodded and smiled.

The lesson? Particularly with annuities, it's important not to substitute a judgment about the intelligence, pleasantness, or competence of an agent in place of an actual reading of the proposed contract and a complete understanding of the charges and fees.

We want to assume that professionals will act professionally, and we want to trust them. Even when we do not, however, we may feel our gap in knowledge means we have no choice but to accept their advice. This is another flavor of substitution bias.

Financial companies know about substitution: they recognize investing clients would rather substitute questions about advisor likability, familiarity, or trustworthiness instead of reading the prospectus. Be mindful of your own substitution tendencies!

Confirmation

Confirmation refers to our Emotional Engine's tendency to listen to statements and facts that confirm our already-held beliefs and ignore facts that refute them. Remember the list of money messages from Chapter 2 that gets posted on the walls in workshops? In one workshop a participant noted, "All the posters say the same thing." (If you review the list you will see one poster says, "There will always be enough," and another one says, "There will never be enough.")

The perception that "all the posters say the same thing" demonstrates our tendency to focus on evidence that confirms what we already believe. The participant was only reading the posters that confirmed her existing values while she was ignoring the others.

When we invest our time or money in a decision, we have a vested interest in being right. We will be receptive to information confirming this belief, and we may not hear or see information to the contrary. To fight this bias, we must vigorously seek viewpoints that are contrary to our own and rationally consider their validity.

Prof. Burton Malkiel, Princeton University economist, is one example. He began researching the effectiveness of passive investing over active investment management in the late 1960s. He has since published 11 editions of his book, **A Random Walk Down Wall Street**, that update his theory with new peer-reviewed studies that continue to test it. His continual search for contrary, consistent proof is a good defense against confirmation bias.

Be cautious of advisors who are unaware that they are subject to confirmation bias. With experience, every advisor develops his or her own unique approach to investing. The more time and money they invest in their own approach, the more they can fall in love with it. Failing to seek new viewpoints can cause them—and their clients—to begin over time to adapt to failure.

Affection

If something reminds us of someone or something else that we like a lot, we will view it as less risky, less detestable, and less of whatever negative qualities it might have. This is referred to as "affect heuristic"—"affect" from affection for something similar, and "heuristic" when it refers to a mental shortcut that employs emotion as a guide to decision-making. In short, we will substitute how we feel about something for what we *think* about it.

A case in point: Delilah had opened an investment account with a large New York bank trust company. She liked her team of professionals so much that she wanted to buy stock in the bank. The excellent service she received from that department, however, had very little influence or reflection on the value of the stock. A few months afterward, the stock was battered by a scandal in a distant department, but the services she received did not waiver.

Another illustration: Physicians with good bedside manners are sued far less frequently than their curmudgeonly counterparts. Does that mean the friendlier doctors are better at practicing medicine? Not necessarily. With many kinds of professionals, we are prone to confusing attitude with aptitude. Should you feel safer with a surgeon you happen to like personally?

An affect heuristic is often behind an individual investor's purchases of stocks in popular retail brands like Apple or Starbucks. It can also explain the placement of unwarranted trust in charismatic but unethical professionals. In making your investment decisions, make sure you detach from any affection you might have developed for the people or the company in question—affection that cannot be backed up by relevant facts.

Overconfidence and Optimism

Overconfidence occurs when we underestimate the odds of a negative outcome. Optimism occurs when we estimate the odds correctly, but believe we will be on the winning side of those odds. Our capitalistic economy is built on our bias toward optimism. If this were not the case, many successful businesses would never even have started up.

Overconfident people may claim that there is less risk in their own personal cases because their skills reduce the risk. Many skydivers, for instance, deny that their sport is risky; to them, it is risky only if one "does not know what one is doing." However, most skydiving accidents are caused by experienced skydivers with hundreds or thousands of jumps. The most common reason: low turn under canopy. In other words, the problem was not the equipment or the weather, but the parachutists' overconfidence in their own skill.

Optimists feel they are especially lucky, believing they can beat the odds. An old finance joke: Many an individual who felt that the odds could be beaten has traveled to Las Vegas in a $15,000 vehicle and come home in a $100,000 vehicle. Sadly, the $100,000 vehicle was a bus.

Even if the odds of success are only ten in 100, our Emotional Engine leads our Rational Engine in thinking that "somebody" has to be in that ten percent, so why not me? rather than realizing that nine times out of ten, the scheme is not successful and the odds improve by walking away. Playing the lottery is the ultimate example of optimism bias at work.

Advisors who are overconfident are often unaware of the magnitude of the risks in the investment product they are recommending. That is why it is important to ask for a prospectus that discloses all possible risks. Ask for the advisor's opinion on the odds of their occurring. By his or her answers, you may be able to better gauge the advisor's awareness and competence in assessing the true odds of success and failure.

Overconfidence and optimism also show up in how we take care of ourselves. When it comes to our health, we may be overconfident about detection and prevention (thus being unable to accurately estimate the odds), but overly aggressive about treatment despite the facts (that is, being given unfavorable odds and continuing to think that we will come out on the favorable side). We tend to think we will not be in the ten percent who get the medical condition, but we also think we will be in the ten percent who benefit from the aggressive treatment. Overconfidence and optimism in their purest forms!

Reluctance to buy insurance sometimes stems from unrealistic optimism. When agents present real data on the probability of a disability, for example, most prospects feel that such statistics don't really apply to them personally. Most of us believe we are less likely than average to die prematurely, be hospitalized, or become disabled. In a study, participants were presented with the statistic that during a given year approximately 19 out of every 1000 persons would sustain an accidental disability lasting more than three months. The group was then asked to estimate their personal odds of sustaining an accidental disability. On average, they felt their personal odds were about six in 1000.

To combat overconfidence and optimism bias, particularly in a large investment decision, it's a good idea to imagine that you've reached a future milestone and the worst possible scenario has unfolded. Spend ten minutes writing down everything that went wrong. Make an honest assessment of the likelihood of each bad outcome, and then revisit your decision.

Be wary of advisors who imply that "it won't happen here," or won't happen to you or to them. Anything's possible. You are far better off to have a professional who over-discloses potential risks than someone who downplays them.

Self-Assessment

*A big decision I am about to make is:*_____

_____

_____

_____

Now speed up the calendar. It's a year later and the worst possible scenario has unfolded. Describe what happened: _____

_____

_____

_____

How likely is each component of my description? _____

_____

_____

Does this exercise help me make my decision? _____

Where are my strengths and weaknesses in dealing with loss aversion, substitution, confirmation, overconfidence and optimism? _____

_____

_____

_____

My Strengths: I act in concert with factual risks rather than using guesswork. One instance where I did so was... _____

_____

_____

My Weaknesses: In the past, I could have done a better job of analyzing risk but I didn't in this case ... _____

_____

_____

_____

Complete these sentences:

I thought I had an ability to predict ... _____

_____

I thought the statistics did not apply to me, but ... _____

_____

I overpaid to avoid a loss by ... _____

_____

What I can do about these is ... _____

_____

_____

_____

2. Media-influenced Mistakes

Certain of our hard-wired biases are exacerbated by exposure to the media.

The Wisdom of Crowds (Not)

When everyone around us appears to be getting rich, it is easy to get swept up in the fervor. Similarly, when crowds are panicking, we have to use every nerve-ending in our Rational Engine to stay on our plan.

In March 2008, six months before the U.S. financial crisis, the Dow was at a record high (again). Howard Marks, chairman of Oaktree Capital Management, aptly described his version of the bull and bear rollercoaster of the markets:

> "Fortunately one of the most valuable lessons of my career came in the early 1970s, when I learned about the three stages of a bull market: The first, when a few forward-looking people begin to believe things will get better; the second, when most investors realize improvement is actually under way; and the third, when everyone's sure things will get better forever.

> "Buying during the first stage can be highly profitable, while buying during the last will carry you over the cliff with the rest of the herd. Relatively few people were eager to buy at the depressed prices of 2002-03. But buying grew in 2004-05 as prices rose and bargains became scarcer, and the pace became fevered in 2006 and the first half of 2007.

> "To aid in your consideration of the future, I've formulated the converse of the above, the three stages of a bear market: When just a few prudent investors recognize that despite the prevailing bullishness, things won't always be rosy; when most investors recognize that things are deteriorating; and when everyone's convinced things can only get worse.

> "Certainly we are well into the second of these three stages. There's been lots of bad news and write-offs. More people recognize the dangers inherent in things like innovation, leverage, derivatives, counterparty risk and mark-to-market accounting. And increasingly the problems seem insolvable.

"One of these days, though, we will reach the third stage, and the herd will give up on there being a solution. And unless the financial world really does end, we're likely to encounter the investment opportunities of a lifetime. Major bottoms occur when everyone forgets that the tide also comes in. Those are the times we live for." [3]

A year after this excerpt appeared, in March 2009, a relatively new client called me on a weekend. She said she had just been watching the news, and she did not think it would be "a good idea" to implement her investment plan right then after all. Her plan called for investing 40% of her all-cash $2 million portfolio in stocks. I asked her to tell me more.

"Well," she said, "Everything I read and everything I hear says that now is the time to be selling stocks, not buying. It's all headed down from here."

"Uh-huh," I replied, "So everybody is saying it's time to sell?"

"Yes!"

I paused and asked slowly, "Which is exactly when you should... what?"

She was silent for a few seconds. Then quietly, she said, "Buy."

I reminded her that we were not going to plunk down the whole 40% at one time. We had arranged a systematic dollar-averaging buying program in chunks with her investment manager to reach her target asset allocation. If the market went down as we were buying, that would actually be a good thing because it would keep her costs low. But if it went up, then she would definitely have bought a good chunk of her long-term assets at a bottom, which is not the overriding goal during implementation, but is certainly a nice bonus.

The next day turned out to be the bottom of that bear market. She still thanks me for that conversation as if I had been a crystal ball reader. Of course, I did not know that we were at the bottom. I just knew, like Howard Marks, about the behavior of crowds and the media during unusual times.

It's worth remembering the words of investor and mutual funds pioneer Sir John Templeton, "To buy when others are despondently selling and to sell when others are greedily buying requires the greatest fortitude and pays the greatest reward."

Availability

One of the most widely studied biases, availability bias occurs when we estimate the odds of an occurrence by the ease with which it can be recalled. We substitute the question of how easily we can remember an event for how often it really occurs.

When I was a kid in the 1970s, we took summer vacations on Florida's west coast, playing on the beach and swimming in the Gulf of Mexico. In 1975 the movie "Jaws" was released. The other kids and I were not allowed to see the R-rated film, but I noticed many more of the adults were not going in the water that year. They even joked that it was because of the movie. Did the chances of a shark attack increase between 1974 and 1975, or did beachgoers just perceive that it did?

What we can easily call to mind tends to be what we are most afraid of, and the more vivid, the greater probability we will assign to it. Journalism exacerbates and plays into this problem. If it is memorable and vivid, then it is news.

Here's an example: Which do you think is more common: homicide or suicide? Few people guess correctly that suicide is seven times more common than homicide. According to the tenets of journalism, most suicides are not newsworthy unless they involve a newsworthy person.

We automatically guess the probability of suicide based upon what we can recall, which presumes that if we have heard about it, it must be more probable.

One subcategory of availability bias is recency bias. The more recently we have heard about something, the more probable we will judge it to be. With recency bias, we tend to over-generalize our previous experience. "It hasn't happened yet, so it probably never will." (As I was happily saying near the end of the third quarter of an historic Tampa Bay Buccaneers vs Tennessee Oilers game, "We've got this one in the bag. I can't ever remember giving up 28 points in the second half of a game." Famous last words for a game that ended in a 31-22 loss to the Oilers.)

The suicide/homicide example also demonstrates how much we rely on the media for our information. Because so much of today's information is unrefined, it is vital to develop our own filters. Spam filters only scratch the surface. What filters are you putting on your television, on your email, on your social media feeds, on your coworkers, on your family? How often do you question where others are getting their information and how rigorously it was tested?

In scholar and philosopher Nassim Taleb's words, "The problem with information is not that it is diverting and generally useless, but that it is toxic... It takes a huge investment in introspection to learn that the thirty or more hours spent 'studying' the news last month neither had any predictive ability... nor did it impact your current knowledge of the world."[4]

Availability bias is both a common and a dangerous influence on our financial decisions. The media can induce panic and fear or greed and excitement that cause people to make irrevocable decisions. There are even "availability entrepreneurs" whose job is to make a minor story seem like major news and then get the story covered by as many news outlets as possible. The public sees the same story on different channels and believes, even though it is from only one source, that the story is utterly true and even more momentous.

Futurist John L. Petersen said, "If you read the entire Sunday *New York Times*, you are assimilating more information than was produced in one year in Thomas Jefferson's time." What if we were as mindful about what we put in our brains as what we put in our mouths? Putting a set of filters in place might be called an "information diet."

A Two-Week Information Diet

For Week #1: Write down every source of information that you receive, and how long you spend with it. Here are some possibilities:

- TV (even if it's in the background)
- Newspapers
- Facebook
- LinkedIn
- Other social networks
- Internet home page (e.g. msn.com or aol.com)
- Internet surfing
- YouTube
- Twitter
- Email
- Magazines
- Lecturer/professor/speaker
- Journals
- Books

- eBooks or Kindle books
- Talking or texting with friends, neighbors, family, and colleagues

Record any time you are awake but not consuming information (exercising, writing, meditating, cooking, hobbies that do not involve reading, watching, or listening to information).

On the seventh day of the first week, answer the following:

For each information source, how conscious was I about selecting what to listen to, watch, or read? _____

_____

_____

What do I think about the quality of the information you absorbed from each source? Was it "empty calories" or nutritional and healthy for me? __

_____

_____

Are there any sources I would now like to reduce my exposure to? _____

_____

_____

What is the ratio of my non-information-consumption time to the rest of my awake time? _____

_____

_____

Imagine I must reduce my information consumption by one-half. What would I definitely keep? What would I get rid of? Why? _____

_____

_____

For Week #2: Focus on information consumption at one-half of your first week's level, concentrating only on the sources most important to you.

Do this by increasing your non-information-consumption time. Find things to do that do not involve consuming information. The toughest part will be keeping conversations to non-information-consumption levels. Talking about the news is verboten; talking about kids and grandkids is great. Use your judgment for times in between. Creating information, like creative writing or creating a YouTube video, is okay as long as it does not involve research.

On the seventh day of Week #2, answer the following:

What did I do with the extra time? _____

_____

_____

_____

How much did I miss the excluded information sources? _____

_____

_____

_____

Do I feel better or worse off as a result? _____

_____

Familiarity

Some people feel safer driving to the airport than flying in an airplane, even though for ten years safety statistics on flying in America have been far better (showing greater safety) than driving. Familiarity bias happens when we believe there is less risk in something familiar than in something unfamiliar.

In order to make things familiar, the media know we like sound bites. One underlying assumption is that if it cannot be simplified into a media-friendly statement, it must be bad. In 2009 in the journal *Psychological Science,* Hyunjin Song and Norbert Schwartz of the University of Michigan found that if participants could not pronounce the name on an amusement park ride and on certain food labels, they perceived them to be more risky. When a simpler, more familiar name was given to the same ride or food, participants thought it was less risky. [5]

Which one sounds like a riskier investment, "a diversified basket of equities and fixed income with a 1% load" or "a 1% fee on a mix of stocks and bonds"? Both describe the same thing. Financial advertisements can make the familiar sound unfamiliar, sometimes heightening an inexperienced person's level of insecurity about investing. To counteract that fear, they offer someone or something familiar—like their brand or message.

It is well known that successful salespeople are familiar faces in their communities. Some have become so for the "right" reasons. Others are showing up in the pond where their target fish are swimming in order to become familiar to those fish. Before checking to see whether someone is competent, we are first attracted to doing business with someone we know personally.

Be cautious of advisors who are unaware that they are subject to familiarity bias. Many professionals choose to receive their education mostly from financial wholesalers, and they begin to develop relationships with them. Because they may like the wholesaler personally, they recommend that wholesaler's products to clients. Professional advisors should provide several choices to clients. Their recommendations should be based upon data provided not only by wholesalers, but by sources such as academic journals as well to counteract their familiarity bias.

Self-Assessment: Familiarity Bias

Strengths: One time when I was uncomfortable with an unfamiliar risk, I sought an objective way to research it and made a decision by... ____

_____

_____

Weaknesses: In my past, I made a decision based upon someone or something that sounded familiar, but I did not check it out thoroughly...

_____

_____

What I can do in the future is... _____

_____

_____

_____

Representativeness

When our Emotional Engine and Rational Engine work well together, we develop intuition. Representativeness bias occurs when we apply intuition in the wrong manner to make important predictions.

The movie "Moneyball" provided a good example of representativeness. A true story about the Oakland As, it begins with the general manager having a scout meeting. The scouts judge potential players based upon the way they look when they hit, throw, and run; the way they act both on and off the field; and even the way they look when they are just standing still. The weight given to the players' actual results is light.

The general manager finds a Yale economics graduate who has studied and charted actual player results. Using his numbers, the team hires a pitcher who throws funny, an almost debilitated hitter, and an outfielder whose sex life makes the papers every day. The scouts scoff. The media pounce. But the team skyrockets.

The scouts are industry professionals. They think they are using valid intuition to make predictions. Yet, they are still highly subject to representativeness bias.

How people and products are staged in the media plays into well-known representativeness biases. As far back as President Warren Harding in the 1920s, looking "presidential" required good height and a square jaw. (President Harding is said to have been elected on these two traits alone.)

The media know we love intuition stories—as when someone, perhaps the hero, "just knew" but did not know how he knew. Intuition stories provide drama, romance, and intrigue—the elements that keep eyeballs glued to the screen. Because our Emotional Engine grasps such vivid emotion, the message to "trust your intuition" is ingrained from our childhood exposure to the media. It is disappointing to learn that our intuition, even intuition from years of specific experience, may not be totally reliable.

In studying different professions, Daniel Kahneman and psychologist Gary Klein, known for his research on firefighters, found that people with the most reliable intuition worked in professions that involved many day-to-day experiences from which they received the quickest feedback. Examples included firefighters and emergency room physicians. The rest were more subject to representativeness, including radiologists (who may not know for months or years if they missed a reading), economists, and investment managers.

Intuition serves us well in fast-moving, dangerous situations like fires and ERs. But most investment decisions are neither fast-moving nor physically dangerous (if you have experiences to the contrary, you may want to write a book). If an advisor ever claims that he or she "just knows," but cannot or will not explain how, then check first for more data, and for representativeness.

Self-Assessment: Representativeness

Strengths: There was a time when I double-checked the intuition I or someone else was using to make a judgment... _____

Weaknesses: There was a time when I went with my or someone else's intuition, instead of double-checking first... _____

What I can do in the future is... _____

3. Mathematical Errors

The third set of common biases stems from our inability to calculate problems more complex than an average, a fraction, or a list more than four items long. We are usually better off using a mechanical calculator than the one inside in our heads.

Linear versus Exponential

Have you ever studied or practiced something every day, but felt you were making no progress, to the point where you became demoralized? We are told that if we practice long enough, we'll one day have a flash of brilliance that brings cohesion to what we have studied.

Leaps in consciousness, on exponential curves of understanding, are natural, but we have trouble projecting exponentially into the future. Journalist, author, and speaker Malcolm Gladwell wrote a book on the subject of these leaps, or "tipping points," and what might predict or predate them. Tipping points come unexpectedly because they defy the immediately prior trend. But tipping points and exponential leaps are far more common than we may believe.

Forecasting and Predicting

In 2005, Lehman Brothers, the now-defunct investment bank, published a housing market forecast with a range of scenarios with probabilities. The "most-likely" scenario gave a 15% probability that housing would rise 11% forever. The "pessimistic" forecast gave a 15% probability of stable prices until 2008 and then a 5% annual increase thereafter forever. The "meltdown scenario," with a 5% probability, forecasted a 5% drop every year until 2008, then a 5% price appreciation would resume in 2009. [6]

Compounding

Compounding means interest accruing on interest. It is one of the most important concepts in finance, and particularly so in investment strategy. Our minds easily grasp the idea of simple interest: you receive or pay a certain percentage of a principal amount. But when we accumulate that interest, add it to the principal, and begin to earn compound interest, our brains give up on the math.

There are several areas where this kind of failure affects our decisions. One is the compounding effect of small losses—namely, taxes, fees and transaction costs. As much as you stand to gain by earning interest on small, repeated amounts of interest and gains on your principal, you stand to lose the same on the small, repeated amounts of taxes, fees, and costs that are deducted from it. The compounded effects of taxes, fees, and charges over a long period can, in some cases, make the difference between outliving your money and not out living it.

In the following example, how much less will David have than Esther?

> Esther starts contributing $2000 a year to her company's 401(k) right after college graduation, at age 22. The investment portfolio she chooses earns 4% for the next 30 years. How much does Esther have when she is 52?
>
> Esther's co-worker, David, waits until he is 37 to start contributing $2000 a year to the same portfolio earning 4%.
>
> How much less does David have than Esther at age 52? Take your best guess.
>
> Because David only contributed for half as long—15 years instead of Esther's 30 years—it would be natural to assume that David will have a little less than half as much as Esther. How much is "a little less"?

Answer: David will have $40,047, just 36% of Esther's $112,170.

How close was your guess?

To appreciate compounding, learn how to use the exponential function on a calculator, or find someone who knows, and take the time to calculate when you see seemingly small percentages accumulating repeatedly on your money over long periods of time. Compounding accurately is key to making more mindful investing decisions.

The Fallacy of Small Numbers: Using a Sample Size of One

In the social sciences, as in economics and psychology, the preferable minimum sample size for a valid study is 25. However, finding 25 observations for some studies can be difficult. In our everyday lives, how many times do we take the trouble to assess and remember 25 observations of anything before we reach a conclusion about it?

Most of the time, we make a judgment about something, or somebody, based upon one observation. When it comes to money decisions, we use first impressions and too-small sample sizes all the time.

Case in point: Robert and I were discussing the percentage of his portfolio that should be invested in bonds, when he interrupted and said, "I bought a bond one time and lost all my money on it."

"You lost all of it?" I asked.

"Yes," he said.

"You mean it went down in value, and you sold it, or the issuer defaulted and you got nothing?"

"The second one."

"Do you remember if it was a junk bond?"

"No, it wasn't. It was a municipal bond."

As we saw in Chapter 5, individual bonds can be excellent sources of principal protection. Less than half of 1% of all municipal bonds default. I have been unable to find a municipal default that returned absolutely nothing to bondholders. But Robert said it happened to him.

When we are the victims of one small investment gone wrong, it can certainly feel as though our chances of repeating it are bigger than they really are. Hiring a professional manager who specialized in municipals and investment grade bonds would have made the chances of a repeat of Robert's experience infinitesimally small. Nevertheless, he was hesitant to invest in any more bonds at all.

On the other hand, advertisers take advantage of our tendency to believe that one-time *positive* events are more repeatable than they really are. Why would any mutual fund advertise its one-year performance, when most funds are best held for longer than one year? Studies of thousands of mutual funds show that the chance of a one-year performance being repeated is very small. The government regulators who oversee financial product advertising require the label, "Past performance is no guarantee of future results." But how much does that label deter the average investor?

An illustration: Brad, an investment manager, was showing me his "trend-following" technique, designed to beat the S&P 500 index by outperforming the index when it goes down. He produced a chart illustrating that $10,000 invested in an index of trend-following managers in 2001 would have beaten the S&P 500 over the ensuing ten years. The chart, which he presumably also showed to prospective clients, showed the trend-following managers handily beating the index. I asked how many trend-following managers comprised the chart. His answer: 20. Statistically speaking, his whole chart was invalid because of the small sample size. Yet few people will think to ask what sample size his figures were based on and will probably give the chart undue consideration.

What can we do instead? The scientific way to use sample sizes in assessing investment strategies would be to examine at least 25 possible outcomes and see how many of them are acceptable. Financial sales and advertising are based upon showing only one historical outcome, knowing we will assume that it will be repeated.

There is a joke in finance: When is a risk not a gamble? Answer: When it turns out in your favor. If we do not understand all of the outcomes that could happen as "risks," we are doomed to failure.

The possible outcomes that do not happen are "alternative sample paths." The alternative sample path is not where you end up at the end of a Las Vegas trip, but how far "up" or "down" you could have been if the trip had ended at any given point in between.

Ideally, we would have at least 25 sample paths to study for each investment decision. This could help us appreciate the degree to which outcomes in financial matters often vary widely and randomly.

Jumping to general conclusions too quickly from small vivid samples is a hard habit to break. Kahneman and Tversky found that even mathematical psychologists, people who should know better, made this mistake.

Self-Assessment: Small Samples

Strengths: A time when I recognized there were not enough observations to make a valid conclusion was... _____

_____

_____

_____

Weaknesses: A time when I made a decision based only upon one observation was... _____

_____

_____

_____

What I can do next time is... _____

_____

_____

_____

Seeing Patterns and Trends in Randomness

If you flip a coin six times, which of the following sequences of heads and tails is more likely to occur:

HHHHHH

HTTHTH

Answer: Both have identical 1-in-64 odds of occurring. One flip's independent outcome does not predict the other.

Why are we inclined to find pictures in clouds and inkblots? We are hard-wired to find *patterns* so that we can use them to make predictions. Predicting accurately has helped us survive and evolve.

When presented with two events, A and B, that appear to be correlated, it is hard not to assume that the correlation will continue. It takes more effort for our brain to reject a hypothesis than to accept it, so once we propose one thing that causes another, we have planted a seed.

Take the "Superbowl Indicator," which showed a correlation between NFC/AFC Superbowl wins and the following year's positive or negative return of the Dow Jones Industrial Average. Our Rational Engine knows that both trends are following independent random patterns, with no causality of one against the other. But our Emotional Engine wants to find causality, patterns, and trends in random events. The media and advertisers play into our presumption of trends and correlations. A headline proclaiming that "A random sensational event happened" is not nearly as compelling or interesting as "A sensational event happened AGAIN. WHY?"

Self-Assessment: Randomness

Strengths: I was able to suspend my tendency to see patterns where there were none when I... _____

_____

_____

_____

Weaknesses: In my past, I made a decision based upon a perceived pattern when I... _____

_____

_____

_____

What I can do in the future is... _____

_____

_____

_____

_____

Elimination versus Reduction of Risk

Because we feel losses more acutely than gains, we mathematically place more value on the elimination of risk than on the simple reduction of risk.

Here's an example: You're facing a chance for a gain of $20,000. You do not know the exact probability. Consider these three pairs of outcomes:

A. The probability is either 0% or 1%

B. The probability is either 41% or 42%

C. The probability is either 99% or 100%

How much are you willing to pay to increase your probability from 0% to 1%, from 41% to 42%, and from 99% to 100%? Research shows that people will pay more to raise the probability of a desirable event for A or C than for B (41% to 42%), even though the increase amounts to 1% in all three cases. When I ask this question in workshops, I get the same responses.

Over-valuing the elimination of risk causes us to overpay for insurance. Commonly, we choose the lowest deductible instead of the highest. We also choose more coverage over less, even when we can afford to self-insure for a portion of the coverage.

Self-Assessment: Risk and You

Imagine that your financial planner shows that you have a 75% chance that you can meet all of your goals at their ideal levels (and a 25% chance of failure), or a 99% chance that you'll meet your goals at their acceptable levels (with a 1% chance of failure).

How comfortable are you with a 25% chance that you may run out of money before your 100th birthday? For most people, this chance is too high.

But what if, by sticking to a 1% chance of failing to meet your goals at their acceptable levels, you must take fewer trips to see your grandchildren?

By experimenting with moving your travel goal off of the acceptable spending level and into the ideal level, you may see a reduction in your odds from 99% to 95%. If a 4% reduction in your odds of success means that you could see the grandchildren more, or take two trips to Europe instead of one over the next ten years, would it be worth the extra risk?

Having a clear understanding of both the acceptable range of risk and your odds of success in insurance and investing will help you to value risk and risk coverage appropriately. Be mindful of your tendency to overpay for elimination of risk, when its reduction may work just fine.

4. Manipulation Biases

The dangerous part about our biases is that when understood well by others, they can be used (unscrupulously) to manipulate our decision-making. Here are some manipulation strategies about which advertisers and financial product pushers are especially keen.

Anchoring

Imagine you received a windfall of $1 million a year ago, but lost $300,000 of it.

Now imagine instead that you received a windfall of $700,000 a year ago, and kept it for a year. Would you feel differently about your financial position in the second case than the first? If so, why?

Anchoring refers to our tendency to find a specific reference point against which to make a judgment or decision rather than letting ourselves start with a blank slate.

Between 2007 and 2011, realtors were frequent witnesses to the unhappy effects of anchoring. Real estate had been appreciating for so long that many sellers were "anchored" to their home's peak value and could not accept the fact that the home was now worth less than their anchored amount. To accept the new market value felt to these sellers like taking a loss, even if the new value was more than the owners paid for the house. Combined with loss aversion, anchoring meant that many owners simply allowed their homes to be foreclosed upon rather than taking offers they considered "low-ball" but that actually reflected current market conditions (and even a possible small profit!).

Anchoring also causes us to look more at percentage differences and relative changes than at *absolutes*. Kahneman and Tversky asked their research subjects what they would do if they set out to buy a $125 jacket and a $15 calculator, and, upon arrival at the main store, the sales clerk informed them that the calculator was now on sale for $10 (a $5 savings) at a branch store 20 minutes away. Under these circumstances, they found that 68% of the respondents were willing to drive the 20 extra minutes to save $5.

In a second version of this inquiry, the $5 in savings was on the jacket price rather than on the calculator—that is, the price of the jacket was $120 at the branch store and $125 at the main store. The price of the calculator was $15 at both stores. The percentage of people willing to drive 20 minutes to save $5 under the second set of circumstances was only 29%.

Either way, $5 would be saved, yet the participants were anchored to the percentage differences in the asking prices, rather than the absolute dollar amounts in question.

Investment advertising and sales take advantage of anchoring by comparing products to an index, and only to those indexes that make the products look good. When we see astonishing performance numbers, particularly when compared to much smaller "benchmarks," they are hard to ignore.

What *should* we anchor to? It depends on the decision to be made, but a rule of thumb is not to anchor at all. Rather, compare the outcomes of the two decision paths to your personal well-being, and choose the more beneficial of the two.

Two Anchoring Couples

During one year following the financial crisis, two different couples in their 60s arrived in my office with the same problem: they both were considering either letting their rental properties go into default and back to the banks, or declaring bankruptcy. Neither couple had had trouble meeting their monthly obligations; both could easily afford the mortgage, taxes, insurance, and upkeep. They were very discouraged, though, about owing more than the properties were worth. The properties had been purchased at a time of escalating real estate values but had not ultimately performed as expected.

They knew that if they defaulted on their mortgages, they would ruin their credit, cause a sudden windfall of income on their tax returns from the forgiven debt, and, most of all I thought, look back with great regret on the fact that they could have met their obligations on their debts but chose not to. Both couples wanted to set good examples for their kids, but neither couple was thinking about the long run, focusing instead only on the short term pain of their dashed expectations. They were both anchoring to the reference points of the properties' peak values and their expectations of perpetual increases.

I asked each couple, "This is a 30-year mortgage. What if your financial plan shows that you would be okay if you pay off the property per agreement over the 30 years? What if, instead of real estate, this was your stock portfolio, the one you expect to *both* rise and fall during the time that you're holding it? Would you have the same trouble holding on to it through this market cycle?"

Because of their high income and their rates of savings, even beyond the debt, both couples were still slated to have a very good retirement life. One couple devised a systematic plan to sell the real estate and come up with any extra equity needed over a ten-year time frame. This couple was relieved to have a decision and a plan, but most importantly, no longer felt anchored to the earlier peak market values and no longer considered walking away from their debts. Both people were looking ahead to their future well-being.

The other couple decided to keep the properties for another ten years and then decide what to do.

To counteract anchoring, get independent appraisals. Accept that market conditions might not be in your favor right now, but they always change. Assess whether the source of your dissatisfaction is temporary or is truly threatening to undermine your long-term well-being. Think in absolute terms that pertain to your unique situation, not in relative terms that pertain to anyone else's. This is another way to stay mindful.

Self-Assessment: To Anchor or Not to Anchor?

Strengths: There was a time when, faced with a decision, I ignored what I had invested and looked only to the future possible outcomes to make a decision about... _____

_____

_____

_____

Weaknesses: In the past, I anchored to an irrational number to make a money decision about... _____

_____

_____

_____

What I can do about it is... _____

_____

_____

_____

_____

Framing or Priming

A type of anchoring manipulation can occur through the use of the framing effect.

"Framing" or "priming" refers to providing a reference point or points in order to manipulate a response. We see this in retail sales all the time: an original price is provided but with a cross-out line through it on the price tag, and a discounted price is shown next to it.

Studies show that the framing or priming of reference points does not even have to seem relevant to be effective. If I asked you how many days it rained in Atlanta last year, and then asked how much you thought my Aunt Millie's lace doily collection is worth, I have already primed and framed your answer to the second question: probably between 90 and 365, with the first question, even though dollars were not the subject. To our Rational Engine, these are two disparate questions. To our Emotional Engine, however, they are the same—both ask us to come up with a number. The tendency to associate similar ideas is irrational, lightning-fast, imperceptible, and unconscious.

Watch for similar framing and priming effects in sales conversations and in advertisements. Many salespeople are trained to bring a high price or other measurement into the conversation so that the "real" amount you might invest or purchase will get adjusted upward in your mind. Stay mindful of your objectives and focused on your plan.

Hindsight

Hindsight bias, as the name implies, is an over-estimation of what we felt we knew at the time. It is the I-knew-it-all-along effect. The danger in hindsight bias is that it causes us to over-estimate our predictive abilities about the future. If we go along with a media commentator's hindsight bias, for example, we might also tend to believe in his or her abilities to predict the future.

When we want to believe that we or someone else has predictive abilities, we often look in hindsight. The problem is, our brains are terrible at remembering facts and circumstances accurately. We remember emotions extremely well, though, and confuse how "clearly" we remember emotions with our clarity about predictions. Unless we have documented proof, we should *not* rely on hindsight alone to determine if we or anyone else has any predictive expertise.

Be wary of advisors who are unaware of their own hindsight biases. They might have a tendency to change their stories to fit their ideas in order to improve their perceived predictive abilities. This is different than admitting that a previous idea has been proved wrong. Practiced, ethical professionals recognize hindsight bias and, rather than change the story, admit their errors.

In 2009, after the financial crisis of 2008, many commentators were proclaiming that they had "predicted" the mortgage meltdown. A Ph.D. student, Dirk Bezemer of The University of Groningen in Holland, analyzed the words of dozens of analysts and commentators to see who actually predicted both the extent and the timing of the crisis.

He found only 12 worldwide who had done so.[7] Subsequently, and ironically, several of those same analysts have made other predictions since then that turned out to be wrong. Rather than trying to find the expert who is the best at predicting the future, you're better off, for a mindful money mentality, accepting that markets and economies are unpredictable. Find professionals who strategize according to this assumption.

Self-Assessment: Predicting the Future

*Strengths: I caught myself believing that I or someone else knew something all along, but then realized I was mistaken when...*_____

_____

_____

Weaknesses: I believed either I or someone else had predictive powers that we really didn't have and made a decision as a result, when... ____

_____

_____

Next time I will act differently and do... _____

_____

_____

_____

Remedies for Natural Emotional Reactions

As you and your planner implement your financial lifestyle plan, the seeds of doubt will inevitably be sown. I find this happens a lot when clients hear about a "new" investment strategy that seems to sound better than the simple one they have used for years.

When things are going extremely poorly for everybody in the stock market, it's hard to resist selling at that most inopportune time. Do not allow the pessimism stampede to sweep you up and carry you along. You must step off to the side and be a spectator at what feels like a financial Armageddon.

Conversely, when things are going well, you will meet someone who is doing even better than you are in some sector or industry or country strategy. The lucrative returns they spout will be a Siren's song to you, urging you to sell your "mediocre" diversified portfolio and switch to this enticing, futuristic, fantastic opportunity. You may hear howls of protest against your simple, boring strategy from people who follow market timing, head-and-shoulder trends, magic Momentum Funds (funds that invest in companies based on current trends), or whatever the latest strategy-of-the-year is. A year or two later their statements may even show that they've earned a lot more than you have. So what? Over time, very few of these strategies work consistently. They have hiccups. When they hiccup, most investors sell under pressure because while the strategies have worked in good times, there is no evidence showing they work in bad times. These investors bail out, ensuring their losses, and look for the next great-sounding thing. The same people who tell 20 friends about their success at making $100,000 may later admit to only one or two friends that they've lost the same $100,000.

Maintaining mindfulness is difficult, but with practice we can become aware of feeling afraid, panicked, greedy, or excited. When you catch yourself in an emotional state over investments, here are four remedies that'll help you stay objective:

1. Remember Hotel California

What's the difference between a German shepherd and a Doberman? German shepherds will not let you into their space, but Dobermans will not let you out. Like the Hotel California lyrics, it's easy to enter into investments that look appealing (you can check in) without looking for the exits (you can never check out).

C.D.s are straightforward: the rate and maturity date are your only concerns. Just because an investment does not have a maturity date, however, does not mean the expected time frame for it is not equally as important. Sometimes we fail to ask what happens if we, or the investment, cannot meet or stick to the maturity date.

To illustrate: Belinda had an opportunity to participate in a real estate swap transaction which would help her avoid a large capital gain on the sale of her office building. The primary attraction of the transaction was the six-figure amount she would save in income taxes. She called to ask me whether anything was wrong with this transaction. Although 6% would go to the agent, with Belinda's income tax savings, it appeared to be a deal too good to pass up.

However, she had not asked what the exit would look like. Once she completed the swap, she would have a new insurance-based investment worth the same as or more than her building, but it was not clear how that investment could be turned into cash other than by her dying and leaving it to her children. Since she was only 52, I asked if this would be acceptable to her. Disappointed, she said it would not.

Even when we understand what the exit or time frame should look like, we often don't take the time to ask what happens if we want to get out earlier. So consider: How severe is the penalty for early withdrawal? Is there a formula for calculating it, or is it dependent upon the market? Is it possible to leave early and make a gain? Is that an appropriate way to view this investment? Is it possible to avoid a penalty if we can find someone to take our place in a partnership? How easily can the investment be turned back into any cash at all?

Why do we seem to concentrate on exit strategies for C.D.s but become less thorough about exits for other investments? Heuristics again: When we do not know what to ask, we shortcut to our emotions: Do we trust this idea or person?

Ask where the exit is and what it looks like.

2. Ask How They Know

How do we know that aspirin is likely to help a headache? Maybe we've tried it before and it worked. But even before that, a scientist at Bayer, say, had tried it and it had worked. The scientist showed it to other scientists who attempted to duplicate and verify the same results. To be extra certain, the scientist also asked his peers to try to prove him wrong; so some of them might have tried aspirin for a headache and found that it didn't work. Because there were peers reviewing the scientist's work, the pharmaceutical company had an accurate idea of both the success rate and the failure rate of aspirin. Bayer was thus able to make an informed decision about whether to proceed with developing aspirin. If aspirin had not been repeatedly tested until it failed, Bayer would not have been confident about investing in it. Just because we don't *know* a failure rate doesn't mean there isn't one.

The same might be said about investment theories. An investment manager might have a theory about growing an investment portfolio by, say, 6% a year. How often do we see the manager asking his peers to duplicate his theory and achieve the same results? How often has the manager asked his peers to prove him wrong? How many of his and similar studies have been published about the theory?

There is no Food and Drug Administration (FDA) equivalent in the financial world. It is up to us to challenge theories we hear about and ask what percentage of the time they don't work. But we're biased! We make investment decisions based on one presentation or sound bite. Be bold and make a habit of asking the presenter, "How do you know?"

3. Popper's Falsifiability Test

Speaking of failure rates, in order to reach a strong conclusion, you must start with a testable hypothesis.

The Falsification Approach was postulated by Sir Karl Popper, a 20th century Austro-British philosopher. It said, "No proposition can be viewed as a scientific proposition unless it can be falsified."

To give some examples, the proposition that "The cure for cancer lies in the ocean" cannot be falsified. We cannot test that there is not a cure for cancer in the ocean; therefore, it is not a scientific proposition.

The proposition that "Gold is cheapest today" cannot be falsified. We cannot test what the price of gold will do in the future; therefore, this is not a scientific proposition.

The proposition that "Over 20-year periods, small cap indexes have had greater volatility and return than corporate bonds" can be falsified. It has been tested many different ways, with varying definitions of "small cap index" and "corporate bonds" and "20 years" (taking the measurements only at the beginning and end of 20 years; or annually every year, or weekly, or daily). This is a scientific proposition from which we can draw some real strategic conclusions. If small cap stocks outperform corporate bonds 90% of the time over any given 20-year period, then when we make a 20-year decision, we have a reasonable expectation (although never complete certainty) of what will happen with small cap stocks relative to corporate bonds. (This is not saying that small cap stocks or corporate bonds are appropriate for your circumstances, however.)

When encountering proposed investing strategies, ask the following:

- Can it be proven false?
- Have any peers attempted to prove it false and failed?
- Have any peers attempted to prove it false and succeeded?
- How often was it false?

What action will you take as a result of accepting or rejecting its truthfulness?

4. Trust Your Instruments

Both aviation and harbor pilots learn to operate and navigate on instruments alone (rather than with the help of visual sightings) in bad weather. I was fortunate to accompany a private pilot and his flight instructor on an airplane instrument lesson on a partly cloudy day in a four-seat Piper Comanche.

After climbing to 5000 feet (verified because I could see the altimeter), the pilot donned "foggles," special goggles that blocked his view of everything except the instrument panel. The instructor then told him to close his eyes while he (the instructor) took over the controls. The instructor made several maneuvers that left me a little airsick. I saw clouds going by and wondered if this was what being in the Space Shuttle felt like—G-forces so strong that I could not lift my head from the back of the seat.

After several seconds of this, the instructor said, "Okay, your airplane." The pilot opened his eyes, saw the panel, and immediately corrected to straight and level. As he did so, I looked for the altimeter, wondering how high we had climbed, and how long it would take to get back down to 5000 feet.

I saw the altimeter, but then I was confused. It said 2000 feet and rising. Did I know how to read the altimeter right? If that reading was correct, then the whole time I thought we were climbing we were actually in a nosedive. Then I doubted the instrument. But both pilots appeared to be confident (but maybe they were both wrong?). A little burst of fear hit my stomach. I looked to see if the ground was racing up at me, but saw only clouds. I was not sure who or what to trust. It was unnerving. But the instrument was correct. My intuition had not been.

Our minds can mess us up in matters of intuition. (I just *knew* we were climbing, right?) Learning to fly by instruments is not so much about learning the instruments as it is about trusting a mechanism and doubting your initial instincts. This is not something that comes naturally to us humans; it requires a lot of practice.

During the financial journey, our minds, the media, our peers, and even our advisors—if they are not the right ones—will distract us with how high or low we are, or how fast or slowly we are going. To filter out the noise, put on *your* foggles and trust your primary instruments: your asset allocation, and the odds of success of meeting your goals.

Notes:

1. Page 144: Daniel Kahneman, **Thinking: Fast and Slow**, (New York: Farrar, Straus and Giroux, 2011), p. 25.

2. Page 151: Daniel Kahneman and Amos Tversky, "Choices, Values and Frames," *American Psychologist*, April 1984, pp. 342-350.

3. Page 164: Howard Marks, "The Tide Goes Out," excerpt reprinted by Peter Lattman at http://blogs.wsj.com/deals/2008/03/20/bull-and-bear-markets-according-to-oaktrees-howard-marks/, March 20, 2008. Used with permission of Howard Marks.

4. Page 166: Nassim Taleb, **Fooled By Randomness: The Hidden Role of Chance in Life and in the Markets**, Penguin Books, 2004, pp. 60-61.

5. Page 170 Hyunjin Song and Norbert Schwartz, "If It's Difficult to Pronounce It Must Be Risky: Fluency, Familiarity and Risk Perception," *Psychological Science,* February 2009, Vol. 20, No. 2, 135-138.

6. Page 174: Paul Willen, "Discussion of 'Investment Dynamics with Natural Expectations,'" *International Journal of Central Banking*, Vol. 8 No. S1, January 2012, p. 269, Table 1.

7. Page 188: Dirk Bezemer, "No One Saw This Coming: Understanding Crisis Through Accounting Models," 2009, Unpublished, The University of Gröningen.

8

Upholding a Mindful Money Mentality

"It's possible to be very active and still not growing or evolving."
~Richard Sincere

Time versus Money

As you begin your journey with your new mindful money mentality, you'll be adjusting to new priorities. Things that once seemed important might not carry so much weight anymore. Other things you might not have thought much about are now front and center. Money might cease to be your primary concern, but another finite resource may well have taken its place: time.

From an economist's viewpoint, time is the ultimate perishable asset. It cannot be saved in a bank account, invested for greater returns later, or transferred to someone who has a deficiency of it. The only way we can make more time, or increase our chances of having more time, is by investing in our health. Other than that, we can only make more life with the time we have. Comparatively considered, money is far more abundant and available to us than time.

You may now be at a place where you are ready to let priorities about time drive your decisions about how to spend, save, invest, and share money. One place to start is with the question, "With whom?" Studies show the happiest people are those with happy relationships. If you were to prioritize whom you would spend your *time with*, rather than your *money on*, who would it be?

Simple Pleasures

After the "With whom?" question, the second most important determinant of our happiness is "How?" And this means how we spend our time, not on one-off fabulous vacations but on everyday exposure to environments and activities that we enjoy.

What small experience do you consistently repeat because it gives you joy or peace? Maybe it's walking your dog. Maybe it's cooking your dinner. Maybe it's going for a swim. But it's some activity that gives you a sense of happiness and can be consistently, frequently repeated in your life. It is something you do solely for the joy it brings you.

Sharing Time

If you find you have an abundance of time, consider sharing it. Reams of data support the notion that giving and volunteering—whether it's money or time—make us happier. Volunteers consistently poll happier than non-volunteers. Givers are far less likely to use self-descriptions like "feeling worthless," "so sad nothing can cheer me up," or "everything is an effort." Communities with the highest percentage of givers and volunteers report higher levels of happiness.

Small, random acts of kindness provide bursts of pleasurable emotions. Blood donors are twice as likely to describe themselves as "very happy" as non-donors are. Teenagers involved in charities have higher self-esteem, fewer pregnancies, and less gang involvement. Senior citizens, given the opportunity to volunteer for six months for a charity, reported significantly higher levels of morale and self-esteem than those who did not volunteer.

Why does sharing our treasure, blood, or time make us feel so much better? Endorphins—chemical messengers of pleasure in our brain—have been shown to be at elevated levels in some volunteers, while stress chemicals like cortisol, epinephrine, and norepinephrine, are shown to be at lower levels.

Another reason charity makes us happier is that it allows us to feel we're in control. Mentoring a teenager, helping a senior citizen with a tax return, or donating to earthquake relief makes us feel as though we ourselves are solving problems. This kind of empowerment is satisfying and long lasting.

Volunteering for something positive takes our minds off of negative events in our own lives. Instead of being stuck in anger and sadness, we engage in healthy, meaningful activities to counterbalance life's bumps along the way.

People who regularly give and volunteer apparently find meaning more regularly in their lives—that is, they make connections between activities with purposeful intent. Regularly engaging the part of our brains attached to meaning produces more life satisfaction.

Self-Assessment: Time

People I want to spend time with include: _____

_____

Simple pleasures I want to continue or start are: _____

_____

_____

Causes I may be interested in supporting are: _____

_____

_____

_____

Your Rights and Responsibilities

By now in our exploration of the mindful money mentality, you now know better than to hold professionals to unreasonable expectations. You know he can neither predict the future, nor guarantee an investment return; you know she cannot guess what you are thinking. You know the planner cannot protect you from the destructive financial habits that you yourself do not address. You know no planner can get you a magical amount of money or consistently "beat the market" every year for the rest of your life. You also know that beating the market is not as important as knowing what you want from your money first.

You also know that once engaged with an advisor, you will both have responsibilities to conduct yourselves according to the standards of a professional relationship. As the client, you have both responsibilities and rights.

Among your responsibilities are:

- To show up: Attend all pre-arranged meetings with all advisors and other professionals (accountant, attorney, trust officer, and others).
- To disclose: Provide complete background information and data so he or she can make fully informed recommendations.
- To communicate: Reveal information about changes in your family situation, including births, deaths, divorces, and marriages of family members.
- To speak up: Ask for clarification when you do not understand.

- To keep up: Reconcile your statements quarterly, or have them reconciled by an independent professional.

- To understand the ways in which your advisors are compensated for the advice they give you.

- To question: Ask why an account or investment is doing so much better than the market just as vigorously as you would question why an account or investment is doing so much more poorly than the market.

- To know: Understand exactly what you are saving and investing for. Know and communicate your personal values, goals, and preferences.

- To know: Know your history with money, money messages, and your susceptibility to certain money issues.

- To do your best to overcome your money weaknesses, and admit when you are having trouble doing so.

Among your rights are:

- To be told the ways in which your advisor can be, is being, and/or could be paid for his/her advice or referrals.

- To have an independent custodian hold your assets and provide you with clear and readable periodic statements.

- To have regular communication (at an interval and format you agree with) regarding your accounts, your financial or estate plan, and significant events.

- To understand your advisor's investment philosophy in words that you can clearly repeat back.

- To be fully informed of your advisor's background, credentials, disciplinary history and business history.

Admitting Mistakes

Maybe you haven't made any mistakes in your financial life. Or maybe, like me, you have. Perhaps, like me, you invested in a friend's startup enterprise that went belly-up. Maybe, like me, you tried to pick stocks and picked the one that ended up under SEC investigation. Maybe, like me, you worked for too long in the wrong job. And maybe, like me, you allowed grief to make you hold on to an inheritance for too long.

I hope you have no experience with any of these mistakes, but if you do, so what? The important question is, did we learn? Is it possible that the mistakes we made and the failures we experienced have made us better humans, after all?

Wherever you are in your financial life, it's the result of many small and large and good and bad decisions you made along the way. You cannot change them, so why dwell on them?

Focus instead on what you can change: every small and large saving, investing, spending, sharing, and hiring decision from today forward. Focus on cultivating new habits and attitudes so those good money decisions become automatic, and you will find yourself dwelling less and less on your money and more and more on your life.

Using the Calendar, Not the News

Remember the work you did in this book! Will your emotions rise and fall with your portfolio, or will you be able to remain rational and stick to your strategy?

The calendar is now your primary investing tool. (Rebalance regardless regularly.) The time to make changes is when the calendar says so or when your planner, on whom you have done your homework and can now trust completely, says so.

Surround yourself with good information, good news, and good people. Maintain your information diet.

How Will You Know You Made the Right Decisions?

Whether you have hired an advisor or are doing your investing yourself, take this test 12 months after implementing your plan. Repeat the test every year and any time you want a self-assessment on your ability to stay mindful.

Self-Assessment: True or False?

_____ *My spouse, children, and I have had healthier, rational conversations about money and our wishes.*

_____ *I am confident that I am going to live a lifestyle conducive to my prosperity, health, and happiness.*

_____ *There are no gaps or overlaps in the advice I have received from my financial advisor, my lawyer, my insurance agent, my banker, and my accountant.*

_____ *When I make a decision to purchase or sell something major, I am confident my financial advisor, accountant, insurance agent, lawyers, and banker are all informed enough to do their parts to make it happen.*

_____ *I completely understand the amounts and ways in which my advisors are compensated, and I feel these are fair.*

_____ *My advisors are at the top of their professions. They are always eager to learn something new in their fields. They are called upon to teach their peers.*

_____ *I never doubt that my financial advisor's recommendations are based solely on what is in my best interests.*

_____ *I am confident my accountant and/or my financial advisor have identified all opportunities for tax savings.*

_____ *It is easy for me to say "No" to unplanned and unwanted charitable solicitations.*

_____ *If I become incapacitated or I die tomorrow, I am not worried about communication between my family and my advisors.*

_____ *I could take a very long vacation with no TV, no phone, and no Internet and not worry about my money while I am gone.*

So how did you do?

If you find a consistent pattern of "False" answers, discuss this with those involved. Ask what they think the problem is and assess whether you should make a change. Planners are not mind readers. When you make your very best effort to be honest with them, they owe you nothing less in return. After all, what are great business relationships built on? Competence, expertise, and integrity in communication.

If I have accomplished anything in this book, I hope it is that I've helped you take stock of your relationship with money, define your destinations for it, implement a roadmap, find a great guide, and enjoy your journey.

I wish you no regrets, good sleep, lifelong success, and peace.

Resources and Reading List

On investigating money messages, beliefs, and habits:

Brent Kessel, **It's Not About the Money: Unlock your money type to achieve spiritual and financial abundance** (New York: HarperCollins, 2008).

Brad Klontz, Psy.D., Ted Klontz, Ph.D., and Rick Kahler, CFP®, **Wired for Wealth: Change the Money Mindsets that Keep You Trapped and Unleash your Wealth Potential** (Deerfield Beach, Florida: Health Communications, Inc., 2008).

Brad Klontz, Psy. D., and Ted Klontz, Ph.D., **Mind Over Money: Overcoming the Money Disorders that Threaten our Financial Health** (New York: Crown Business, 2009).

Syble Solomon, Money Habitudes: **A Guide for Professionals Working with Money Related Issues** (Wilmington, NC: LifeWise Productions, 2009).

Lynne Twist and Teresa Barker, **The Soul of Money: Reclaiming the Wealth of Our Inner Resources** (New York: W.W. Norton, 2003).

Susan Zimmerman, **The Power in Your Money Personality: 8 Ways to Balance Your Urge to Splurge with Your Craving for Saving** (Beaver's Pond Press, 2002).

On money imbalances and/or disorders:

Drs. Klontz: www.YourMentalWealth.com

Financial Therapy Association (www.financialtherapyassociation.org)

Dr. Mary Gresham - www.atlantafinancialpsychology.com

Olivia Mellan – www.moneyharmony.com

On money and happiness:

Arthur Brooks, **Gross National Happiness: Why Happiness Matters for America – and How We Can Get More of It** (New York: Basic Books, 2008).

Ed Diener and Robert Biswas-Diener, **Happiness: Unlocking the Mysteries of Psychological Wealth** (Malden, MA: Blackwell Publishing, 2008).

Vicki Robin, Joe Dominguez, and Monique Tilford, **Your Money or Your Life: 9 Steps to Transforming Your Relationship with Money and Achieving Financial Independence** (New York: Penguin Books, 2008).

On money messages:

www.moneyhabitudes.com - Website with card and workbook tools to explore money beliefs and behaviors

www.mindfulfinancialplanning.com - Website of Susan and Steve Zimmerman, experts on money personality and applying money messages in financial planning

On getting out of debt, overspending, or saving too little:

Dave Ramsey, **The Total Money Makeover: A Proven Plan for Financial Fitness** (New York: Thomas Nelson, 2004).

Local, not-for-profit credit counseling services (check with United Way - do not use for-profit credit counseling until you have tried a not-for-profit one first)

www.smartypig.com - an online bank account that allows for savings "buckets" within the same account.

On tracking expenses:

Kenneth Robinson, **Don't Make a Budget: Why It's So Hard to Save Money and What to Do About It** (Columbus, OH: SPS Publications, 2010).

www.aadmm.org - Website of American Association of Daily Money Managers

www.welovethezero.com - Website of Beth Crittenden, financial organizer

www.mint.com - Has apps for mobile devices so you can track expenses real-time

www.vitalfinancials.com - Website of Natalie Wagner, cash flow consultant

www.quicken.com - If you want to download data to a program on your computer

On long-term care insurance:

www.aarp.org - Website of the American Association of Retired Persons

www.llis.com - Website of Low Load Insurance Services - (You must have a referral from a planner to obtain a long term care insurance quote. If you do not have a planner yet, use "Holly Thomas - Mindful Money Mentality" as your planner referral. No compensation is paid from Low Load Insurance to referring planners.)

On end-of-life planning:

Lewis Walker, **Planning for the Challenges of Aging, Healthcare, and Special Needs** (Denver: FPA Press, 2012).

www.YourCareJourney.org - Website of the Advanced Care Coalition for patients diagnosed with terminal illness and their families

www.forbes.com/sites/carolynmcclanahan - Carolyn McClanahan, M.D., CFP® blogs on money and medicine, including end of life issues

On ethical wills:

www.personallegacyadvisors.com - Website of Susan Turnbull, writer and specialist in documenting family histories

For a more holistic perspective on estate planning, consider legal, accounting, and/or financial members of the Purposeful Planning Institute (www.purposefulplanninginstitute.com).

On thinking more positively and appreciatively:

www.edwardjacobson.com - Website of Dr. Edward Jacobson, expert in appreciative inquiry

www.drpaulwhite.com - Website of Dr. Paul White, psychologist

On background checks and disciplinary history:

1. Your state regulator. Search for the department of financial services, or office of financial regulation for your state, or you can find the link at the website of the North American Securities Administrators Association (www. www.nasaa.org). You will find ADVs for small Registered Investment Advisors (RIAs) there, and for RIAs who do not manage money.

2. www.sec.gov. Larger RIAs who manage more than $100 million are required to be registered with the SEC.

3. National Association of Insurance Commissioners (www.naic. org). At the link for your state's website, you will find anyone who is licensed to sell any insurance products, including annuities.

4. FINRA's BrokerCheck (http://www.finra.org/Investors/ ToolsCalculators/BrokerCheck/). Here you will find a background check on anyone who holds a Series 7 license and/or is employed by or owns an RIA.

On behavioral economics:

Daniel Kahneman, **Thinking: Fast and Slow** (New York: Farrar, Straus, and Giroux, 2011).

Steven D. Levitt and Stephen J. Dubner, **Freakonomics: A Rogue Economist Explores the Hidden Side of Everything** (New York: William Morrow, 2006).

Nassim Nicholas Taleb, **Fooled By Randomness: The Hidden Role of Chance in Life and in the Markets** (New York: Random House, 2005).

Carl Richards' blog – www.behaviorgap.com

Other books:

Stuart E. Lucas, **Wealth: Grow It. Protect It. Spend It. And Share It.** (New York: Pearson Prentice Hall, 2006).

Twitter:

@carolynmcc - An M.D./CFP® tweets on money and medicine
@hollypthomas – Author's blog on money and happiness
@behaviorgap - Carl Richards on behavioral finance

LinkedIn groups:

Mindful Money Mentality - community for book readers and mindful financial planners

Purposeful Planning Institute - community for purposefully-minded attorneys, accountants, and financial professionals

---

Neither Porchview Publishing, LLC, Holly P. Thomas, nor Holly P. Thomas, LLC received, nor will receive, any compensation from these resources in return for their listings here.

Fiduciary Oath

National Association of Personal Financial Advisors

The advisor shall exercise his/her best efforts to act in good faith and in the best interests of the client.

The advisor shall provide written disclosure to the client prior to the engagement of the advisor, and thereafter throughout the term of the engagement, of any conflicts of interest, which will or reasonably may compromise the impartiality or independence of the advisor.

The advisor, or any party in which the advisor has a financial interest, does not receive any compensation or other remuneration that is contingent on any client's purchase or sale of a financial product.

The advisor does not receive a fee or other compensation from another party based on the referral of a client or the client's business.

Following the NAPFA Fiduciary Oath means I shall:

·   Always act in good faith and with candor.

·   Be proactive in disclosing any conflicts of interest that may impact a client.

·   Not accept any referral fees or compensation contingent upon the purchase or sale of a financial product.

Signed this _____ of _____

_____

NAPFA-Registered Financial Advisor

NAPFA
THE NATIONAL ASSOCIATION OF PERSONAL FINANCIAL ADVISORS

DISCLOSURE FORM INSTRUCTIONS

The purpose of this document is to provide full and specific disclosure as to how the financial planner and the planning firm will be compensated if the client decides to accept and implement the planner's recommendations.

The form is divided into three sections. In the Investment/Insurance Products section, the planner indicates the recommended product, the recommended amount to invest or purchase, and the estimated commission rate and amount that will be received by the planning firm and all affiliates. In the Services section, the planner indicates the estimated income to be received by the firm and all affiliates from the services suggested. The third section, Other Compensation, requires an explanation of other forms of compensation the planner and planning firm may receive as a result of the planner's recommendations. Definitions of the terms used in this section are provided on the back of this form.

Generally, the planner will provide an estimate of expected income to the firm and all affiliates because exact amounts may be unknown at this time. However, the planner should specify amounts to as great a degree of accuracy as possible. Both the planner and the client should be able to rely on this document if there is a question about whether the planner made a good-faith effort to fully disclose compensation.

Both the client and the planner should sign this form. The client should receive a signed copy.

The National Association of Personal Financial Advisors (NAPFA) is the primary professional organization for financial planners who have agreed to work only on a fee-for-service (Fee-Only) basis. Members must adhere to strict professional standards. They may not receive any commissions or other economic benefit, other than fees paid by the client, from their clients' implementation of their recommendations.

NAPFA members believe that full disclosure encourages greater professionalism among advisors, discourages them from self-dealing, and gives consumers greater power throughout the planning engagement. Disclosure gives consumers the information they require to make informed decisions ***before*** they implement product recommendations. NAPFA has received the support of the AARP, Consumer Federation of America, and several state regulators for its efforts on the disclosure issue. For more information, write:

NAPFA
3250 N. Arlington Heights Road, Suite 109
Arlington Heights, IL 60004
847-483-5400

NAPFA
THE NATIONAL ASSOCIATION OF PERSONAL FINANCIAL ADVISORS

Learn more at www.NAPFA.org

SAMPLE

Definitions

12b(1) Fees: These are charges deducted from your investment mutual fund.

Trailing Commissions: These are the amounts paid by the insurer to the planner and/or the planning firm for each year that you own an insurance policy. Referral fees are another form of trailing commission. Typically, referral fees are paid by an outside vendor for the planner's referral of your business. The planner may earn a fee, similar to a trailing commission, for each year in which you are invested with the outside vendor.

Surrender Charges: This is a charge deducted from the balance in your annuity policy or insurance contract if the policy is cashed-in or surrendered early. These charges apply primarily to insurance and annuity products and may vary from product to product. A portion of the surrender charge is used to reimburse the insurer for the commissions paid to the planner at sale.

Back-End Fees: Similar to a surrender charge. An amount deducted from the balance in your investment if the investments is sold early.

Contingency Fees: A payment that is contingent on certain events. For instance, the panner of planning firm earns a payment only if they can find a buyer for the non-performing investment property.

Eligibility for Sale Prizes: The planner qualifies for additional compensation if a certain level of sales of a specific product is reached.

Soft-Dollar Benefits: The planner, or planning firm, receives compensation, not in the form of cash, but in the form of other benefits. Among other things, "soft-dollar" benefits might include a subscription to the *Wall Street Journal*, a new computer, or payment for training programs for staff.

Performance Compensation: Compensation is contingent on reaching certain performance objectives. For example, if the investment earns 10 percent, the planner or planning firm may earn .5 percent, but if the investment earns 20 percent, the planner or planning firm may earn 3 percent.

This Compensation Disclosure Form has been copyrighted by and is being used with the permission of the National Association of Personal Financial Advisors. Making copies of this form is prohibited. To purchase reprints of this form, contact NAPFA at 847-483-5400

Disclosure of Financial Planner Compensation

For the period _____ to _____

Investment and Insurance Products	Amount to Invest	Estimated Commission Rate	Estimated Income to Planning Firm and Affiliates*
_____	$_____	_____%	$_____
_____	$_____	_____%	$_____
_____	$_____	_____%	$_____
_____	$_____	_____%	$_____
_____	$_____	_____%	$_____
TOTAL	$_____	_____%	$_____

*Total amount of commission, rebate or fee typically earned by the planner, firm, employee and affiliate in the first year.

SERVICES: Incl. Money Management, Investment Supervision, Retainer Arrangements or Implementation Fees

_____	$_____
_____	$_____
_____	$_____
TOTAL	$_____

Other Compensation to Planning Firm and Affiliates (Check all that apply and explain to client)

	No	Yes		No	Yes
12b(1) Fees			Eligible for Sales Prizes		
Trailing Commissions			Soft-Dollar Benefits		
Surrender Charges			Performance Comp.		
Back-End Fees					
Contingency Fees					

Note to client: Estimated commissions and fees do not include commissions and fees that might be payable to non-affiliated third parties as a result of the purchase of financial products or services. These commissions and fees may be substantial. The client is strongly advised to seek full disclosure of fees and commissions when purchasing financial products or services.

I acknowledge receiving this document:

_____	_____	_____	_____
Client (signature)	Date	Client (signature)	Date
_____	_____	_____	_____
Planner (signature)	Date	Principal (signature)	Date

SAMPLE

For more copies of this book, order on Amazon.com or send a check for $17.95 plus $7.00 for shipping ($24.95) to:

Porchview Publishing LLC

2202 N West Shore Blvd., Suite 200

Tampa, FL 33607

For upcoming Financial Lifestyle Planning Workshops, or to schedule a Financial Lifestyle Planning Workshop for your group or client group of 8 or more people, email: porchviewpublishing@gmail.com

---

Financial professionals interested in bulk purchase of this book, or client group sessions on individual book topics, email holly@hollypthomas.com or call 813-489-1700. State your name, location, and a good day and time to contact you.

Acknowledgments

I was fortunate to have a family of cheerleaders for this book. I would not have seen this through to completion without my husband Skip's confidence and encouragement. Mom, Laura, and Jill were always supportive and eager to help and read numerous drafts. My gratitude also goes to Sue Green; and to my father—even though he never saw the first draft, I still feel his confidence in me.

Numerous friends contributed constructive ideas and frank feedback, especially Terry Lubotsky; Jennifer Lazarus, CFP®; Judy McNary, CFP®; and Rose Brempong. I owe thanks for support and accountability to John E. Nelson and Kathleen Rehl, Ph.D., CFP®.

To Richard Sincere; Dr. Ted Klontz; Syble Solomon, Ph.D.; Jeff Daniher, CFP®; David Jacobs, Ph.D., CFP®; MaryAnn Hoffman; and Andrew Dougill; Jerry Skapyak; Ken Donaldson, LMHC; and Dr. Dae Sheridan—I owe thanks for reviewing and providing feedback on quotations, sections, or chapters. Their efforts vastly improved the book's accuracy and readability. Any remaining errors are entirely mine.

For quotation permissions, thanks to Bob Veres, Richard Sincere, Mitch Anthony, and Howard Marks.

Thanks go to Barbara Escher, who was the first person I believed when she said I had a book in me. Francie King's extensive editing and proofreading polish brought sparkle to very rough drafts. Thanks also to editor Deborah Bancroft. They all contributed to eliminating the unnecessary so that the necessary could speak.

Jenna Kusmierek's design produced a book more beautiful than I ever imagined.

Finally, I thank each and every one of my banking and planning clients for the past 25 years. Without you, I would not have learned the life lessons this book endeavors to share.

"Each indecision brings its own delays and days are lost lamenting over lost days... What you can do or think you can do, begin it. For boldness has Magic, Power, and Genius in it."
~ Johann Wolfgang von Goethe

Made in the USA
Lexington, KY
07 April 2014